The Writer's Guide to Query Letters and Cover Letters

Gordon Burgett

Prima Publishing
P.O. Box 1260B3
Rocklin, CA 95677
(916) 786-0426

Typography by Coghill Book Typesetting
Copyediting by Ruth Cottrell
Production by Janelle Rohr, Bookman Productions
Cover design by The Dunlavey Studio

Library of Congress Cataloging-in-Publication Data

Burgett, Gordon, 1938–
    Writer's guide to query letters and cover letters / Gordon Burgett.
        p. cm.
    Includes index.
    ISBN 1-55958-118-2
    1. Queries (Authorship) 2. Cover letters. I. Title.
PN161.B84   1991
808'.066—dc20   91-20078
                                                            CIP

92 93 94 95 RRD 10 9 8 7 6 5 4 3 2

Printed in the United States of America

How to Order:
Quantity discounts are available from Prima Publishing, P.O. Box 1260B3, Rocklin, CA 95677; telephone (916) 786-0426. On your letterhead include information concerning the intended use of the books and the number of books you wish to purchase.

U.S. Bookstores and Libraries: Please submit all orders to St. Martin's Press, 175 Fifth Avenue, New York, NY 10010; telephone (212) 674-5151.

DEDICATION

To Shannon and Kim, whose teen and college years were spent waiting for the windfall from my "query books." They are wiser now and even more lovely. Since the earlier editions kept them in cars, such as they were, this one is to keep my truck running.

CONTENTS

PREFACE

Query letters are the difference between the amateur and the professional in the writing world. They get your ideas and words in print quickly, surely, and with a minimum of wasted time and effort.

Cover letters are their counterpart in the reprint and simultaneous submission fields. They help you sell that first article again and again, or to many markets in the right fields at the outset.

Whether your words see print for pay or you get another exasperating rejection rests solely with the editor. This book describes these tools; it shows how professionals deal successfully with editors and how you can do the same throughout your writing career.

It's really that simple. You know something that others should know. But you may not know how to share that something—a fact, an idea, a feeling—with others in print. And even if you write like Shakespeare (or Jorge Amado), what you have to say won't be published until you can get an editor to give you the nod.

In 1980 I wrote *The Query Book* to help you, and others like you, bridge the gap of getting in print, as professionals do, with query letters. A well-written query is almost negotiable tender. But it must be done right.

Five years later I wrote a second edition of that book, called *Query Letters/Cover Letters: How They Sell Your Writing*, and added another 100 pages about cover letters.

For that edition, I also asked editors from various publications to share their ideas about queries, and those comments were so instructive that I have kept them for this book, which expands and updates my previous books. You'll see that there's not much difference between what I write and what they want. Nor has it changed a whit in the past 5 years—or 20.

The 10 examples each of query and cover letters from the previous editions have been added to this version because I feel it is important to share both my thoughts and the corresponding examples at various stages of my own selling growth. But I've edited and updated much of the support text and have included 10 more recent query letters to provide you with 30 examples to use as needed. Beyond that, your own wit and skill will carry you through.

You see, if you're smart and literate and write copy that is good enough to be printed, it won't take you long to catch on to querying and then following up (when needed) with cover letters. But they're not magic. They don't substitute for clear thought, tight editing, and persistence. They do let you compete like a professional from the first venture, though, and they'll keep you earning regularly and reliably until you put your pen or disk to rest.

When I wrote the first edition of this book, I had been in print some 350 times. Since then I've had about 700 more items published. It's not the writing that makes the difference. My writing is probably at a par with yours. It's the way I market. It's the fact that I do precisely what I'm telling you how to do on these pages. And if it works for me, it will work for you!

There's nothing mystical about writing. It's hard work. But the rewards far outweigh the toil and testing. And anyway, we need to know what you have to say. You're important and it's important. It matters to me that you have a chance to help all of us learn more. So get reading, then get writing. We'll see you soon in print!

PART ONE

What This Book Is All About

CHAPTER 1

The Letters, the Editor, You, Selling, and Time

You want to write for a living? Great! The writing part is easy enough—you've been doing it since you were a kid.

Just think of how many times you've read something and said, "I can write better than that!"

You probably can, or soon could with practice.

But can you do it regularly? Can you live on that income? It's the "for a living" part that separates the wishers from the doers. And that depends on how you use your time.

For years I taught a class called "How to Sell 75% of Your Freelance Writing," and now I offer that material as a seminar and through a book by a similar name. The title is a mouthful, but it's right on target. If you sell much less than 75% of what you write, you can't make it professionally, or for a living.

This book guides you through the two most important elements of selling your writing.

First, it discusses the querying process. It covers

the few and scattered points made in other literature about querying and adds substantially to them. Sample query letters are included, in part to make up for their scarcity elsewhere.

Second, it shows you how and when to write cover letters, with examples. Thus it discusses the two key marketing tools that all writers need to know about and use: queries, sent before you write the copy, and cover letters, which accompany copy already written.

THE QUERY LETTER

A query letter, in a sentence, is a letter sent to an editor asking if he or she would be interested in (buying) an article about a particular topic. But it isn't quite that simple.

How long should the letter be? What must it contain, and what should it never say? To whom should it be sent? When will that person reply? What happens if he or she doesn't? Why not query by phone? And isn't it far more efficient to send the same letter to a dozen editors and then write for the one who promises to pay the most?

THE COVER LETTER

A cover letter accompanies a manuscript or copy. It's usually short and to the point: Is the editor interested in using the enclosed material? Once again, it's not that simple.

Why are you sending the copy? Why aren't you querying instead? Has the piece been in print before? Are photos available? What rights are you offering? What are your qualifications? And more.

For both query letter and cover letter, there is a need for a general grasp of the relationship among the letter, the editor, you (the writer), a professional selling process, and time. Such an understanding puts the most important element—the writing—into its proper perspective.

WHAT YOU REALLY SELL

What you sell in print is time. The time it takes you to think of something to write about that others want to read, test the topic to see that it can be written about, identify markets, find an interested editor, complete the research, write, edit, submit, sell, and resell.

Those who can do this quickly and well get the biggest rewards: fortune and fame. The fortune will be modest, at least at the outset. The fame will be even more modest. The key word is *quickly*. Worse yet, if you don't do every aspect of this process *well*, you probably won't be in print at all.

Thus what you want to do is what every professional does: Find the fastest and most efficient way to reduce time-taking risks and increase the profitability of every moment used. That's where query and cover letters fit in. Without them, you are reduced to groping in the dark, losing days and months trying to match ideas, words, and hope to print dollars. With them, you zero in on markets and reduce the groping and loss. The crucial tool is the query. Then you multiply one sale into many with the cover letter.

So let's focus primarily on the query here, mentioning the cover letter only when it is appropriate. We concentrate on it later.

HOW TO PREPARE AND MARKET ARTICLES THAT SELL

When you write an article for a magazine you can either write the copy and send it to the editor, as many novices do, or you can ask the editor first if he or she would be interested in reading and using the article when you have written it. Professionals do the latter, though there are exceptions, which I will explain later.

The first approach assumes either that you have infinite time and extraordinary skills to turn out many, many super articles or that you are psychic and thus know what each editor needs. Unless the latter is true, in which case you'd get far richer simply selling that knowledge to other writers, you will wind up spending 90% of your time writing, typing, editing, and rewriting to sell maybe 5% or 10% of what you produce.

That's foolish. Professionals can't survive on publishing's meager returns unless they sell at least 75% of their work—and most easily top 100%, with simultaneous submissions and reprints. They write a one-page letter—a query—and write the article only when the editor gives them a positive, "let-me-see-it" response. Then they resell the sold item, through cover letters, time and time again.

This process is the step-by-step theme of another of my books, *How to Sell More Than 75% of Your Freelance Writing.* Query letters, and then cover letters, are the tools that distinguish amateurs from professionals and make that 75% selling ratio possible.

The book you are reading expands the discussion and presentation, through examples, of each of those elements.

Yet to put query and cover letters into perspective,

let me borrow a 15-step guide from *How to Sell More Than 75% of Your Freelance Writing:*

1. In one sentence, what is the subject of the article you want to write and sell?

2. Who will benefit from reading your article? Who will be most interested? What kinds of readers will select your specific subject from a variety of choices? Rank all of those potential readers in order, placing those who will derive the most benefit first.

3. Which publications do these readers buy and read? Prepare a market list of those publications that are the most likely to buy your manuscript.

4. In addition to the publications checked in (3), it is necessary to review the broader publishing field for articles similar or identical to yours. Therefore, you must check both the *Reader's Guide to Periodical Literature* and the specific subject indexes for at least three previous years, then

   a. list the articles that are closest to your subject, in order, with the most similar first: subject, author, title, publication, page reference, length, and date of publication. When the subjects appear to be very similar, how does yours differ?

   b. cross-check newspaper indexes for the past three years and list the same information.

5. Have the publications in (3) and (4) printed articles similar to the one you propose within the past three years?

6. After each publication, note the name and title of the person you should contact (editor, man-

aging editor, etc.), and address. Then note the following information about each publication:

a. Does it pay on acceptance or publication?

b. How much does it pay for articles as long as yours?

c. Does it prefer a query or a direct submission?

d. How often is it published?

e. What percentage of it is written by freelancers?

f. What is its preferred manuscript length?

g. Is any other information provided that will affect its placement on your list?

7. Now rank your market list in priority order, based on when the buyers pay (on acceptance or on publication), how much, the frequency of publication, and the percentage of freelance material used per issue.

8. Read the latest issues of your target publication, front to back. Select the articles that are the most similar, in form if not topic, to the piece you are planning. Outline each article. Write out the lead and conclusion of each, by hand. Attempt to identify the publication's readers by age, sex, occupation, income range, education, residence, and other pertinent factors.

9. To verify the availability of resource information

a. read as many of the articles in (5) as necessary or possible and then list the sources of information found in each.

b. consult your library's card catalogue and list books you will refer to for factual information: title, author, call number, date of publication.

c. list the people you should consult for additional information and quotes, working with the reference librarian for information that you do not already have: their names, positions, current affiliations (if relevant to the topic), academic titles and degrees (if relevant), and reasons for consulting them.

10. From the information you've gathered on the specific target publication and the research you've done on your topic, select the material you need to write a professional query letter. Verify its accuracy.

11. Write a selling query letter to an editor of your target publication. If you do not receive a positive reply, write a query letter to the editor of the next publication on your list, and so on, one editor at a time, until an editor does respond positively. Repeat as much of (9) as necessary for each new publication queried.

12. When you receive that positive response to your query, complete the plan for your article to determine what is still needed to finish it.

13. Complete the needed research.

14. Write the manuscript in final draft form. Include, on a separate sheet of paper, at least five additional, different leads.

15. Select the best lead, edit the draft, type a final manuscript, photocopy it, and mail the manuscript with illustrations (if available and needed), to the editor who gave you the go-ahead.

Ten of the 15 steps precede the query letter. You must first find something to write about and then decide whether it's feasible to complete an article about that topic and whether there are markets with readers eager for your information.

Then you query. You send a letter to the editor of the most likely publication. If you get a negative reply, you try the second editor, and go down your list, one at a time, until a publishing genius recognizes your talents as well as a gripping topic and says, "Yes, I'll look at it!" Only then do you fully research, interview, photograph, and write.

The details about the querying process are explained in the chapters that follow. But first let me add a few thoughts about the general topics of writing and selling before we look at an actual query letter.

WRITING

Most beginners eager to be in print put too much emphasis on writing skills and pay too little attention to selling, in part because selling is so poorly explained in the books they have at hand.

Yet the actual writing, the formation of phrases and paragraphs around thoughts, is of little mystery to a literate person. In fact, if you can wrap four good sentences around a thought, and do that consistently, you can be a selling writer.

Three skills are crucial: clarity, brevity, and flow. If you can present an interesting idea clearly and briefly, and if your presentation flows smoothly and sensibly, about all that is missing is an interest-grabbing lead, a conclusion, and factual accuracy.

You can read books about each of these elements, and more. Better yet, read the articles in the publications in which you want to appear and focus on each until you see how the writer has treated the subject and why the article is in print.

Writing is like swimming. It takes a bit of practice to coordinate the motions but once you have learned it, you never unlearn it. In both, the more you practice, the better you get. In swimming, you may eventually want to study with a master. In writing, you can pick up almost any good book or article and learn from it. The rest is putting the learning on paper.

In summary, if you can write as well as the articles already in print in your target publication, if your query letter gets you a chance to submit your work for serious consideration by that publication, and if your article is then accepted, what more can you ask? Only that it be printed again, by others. Do that often enough and you will be writing for a living.

SELLING

Most writers shake in fear of what they suspect are their writing inadequacies. They are shaking for the wrong reason. What they usually can't do is sell. Not that they are incapable of selling themselves or their copy, they just don't know how. If they did, they'd see that selling would force them to improve their writing skills to meet their querying promises.

In principle, selling your writing is simple. You convince an editor hundreds or thousands of miles away that you have an exciting idea that his or her magazine needs because it tells the readers something they want to know but don't. What's more, you are the person who should tell them. Finally, the editor can see by the lively, bright, clear, concise prose in your one-page letter that you can write. In fact, all that's missing is a go-ahead and you'll have a blue-ribbon manuscript in his or her hands pronto. (The "great piece!" note and check will quickly follow.)

That's what a query letter should do.

You see where the writing fits in. Unless your query is well-written, unless it reads as smoothly as the copy in the publication and convinces the editor that you can present ideas clearly and fully, that editor will not ask to see your manuscript. There are too many query letters on the editor's desk that *do* those things for the editor to gamble on you. So your query must be well-written. Then you must follow it up with a manuscript as good as the query.

In trying to live up to these expectations, you will either meet the demands or you will not write for a living. Cruel, but true.

Do you see why I say that selling or marketing is the first and most important step, and that writing follows obediently behind like an eager puppy?

The responsibility of this book, then, is clear: to show you what a query letter looks like, what it must contain, when and how it should be sent, and a multitude of other nuances that may mean the difference between not writing for sale at all, writing and selling now and then, and writing for a living. Then, later, to show how the cover letter extends the life and sales power of an item already written.

Let's answer the question, "What is a query letter?" in the next chapter and then look at an actual query letter in Chapter 3.

———■———

I get scores of manuscripts each year not even remotely relative to the editorial needs of our magazine. Why a writer would waste the time, effort, and postage in submitting a full-length manuscript, perhaps even with photos (in focus or not), without first determining if we could use it is beyond me.

Bob Kleinfelder, senior editor, The Lion Magazine *(Lions Club International)*

PART TWO

Query Letters— Articles

CHAPTER 2

What Is a Query and What Should It Say?

A query, in simplest terms, is a question, an inquiry. For nonfiction freelancers, querying is most often done by a letter built around the phrase, "Would you be interested in . . . ?" Its purpose is to interest editors in ideas they will use in their publications.

Not all queries should be made by letter. Some are better done by phone or in person, and we will discuss those later. Writers thinking of querying by other, more exotic means are left to their own designs, with the question, "Why?"

Some elements must appear in every query letter: what you want the editor to consider, your name, and how you can be contacted. Thus a letter asking for editorial or writer's guidelines, while a good idea before querying, is not a query. Nor is a letter asking an editor what is needed—a letter to be avoided because it shows that you have no concept of what a writer should do: provide both ideas and manuscripts.

Query letters commonly include some mention of

your published credits, your special preparation or expertise in dealing with the topic, the sources that will be used, perhaps the names of those to be interviewed, the type and quality of illustrations to be submitted with the manuscript, and enough factual material about the topic to convince the editor that readers would benefit from and enjoy reading your article.

Freelancers want to sell their writing; editors need to buy good copy to fill their pages. The query letter is a timesaver that lets you, the writer, test an idea before having to complete the research, conduct interviews, take photos, and write the manuscript. Instead, you briefly research your idea to see whether a full piece can be written about it and your thesis supported. When you are certain that an article is worth writing and can be written, you write a query letter asking if the editor would be interested in using such an article in his or her publication.

The editor doesn't know at this point whether you have written the article or are about to do so, and he or she can only assume that if you speak of it as a reality, the manuscript will be delivered as promised.

Based on that assumption, the editor responds, telling you to

1. mail the manuscript and expect a check to be sent, now or upon receipt, for its purchase;
2. mail the manuscript on speculation, which means that if the editor thinks the final piece, once read, can be used, as is or with alterations, a check will follow;
3. wait, usually citing some reason for delaying full consideration of the idea;
4. not send the manuscript, rejecting it with a per-

sonal comment or explanation why it can't be used; or

5. not send the manuscript, rejecting it without a personal comment, often on a mass-produced form.

The first possibility—a purchase, sight unseen—is highly unlikely unless you have sold to a market repeatedly or unless you have a reputation that assures you or your agent some form of advance payment. Possibility (3) is equally unlikely. Editors usually either pass judgment on the labors of newcomers to the writing world before giving them the nod or turn them down. Good query letters usually save you from the dehumanizing fate of (5), and they frequently move you from (4) to (2) on your second or subsequent query. An initial idea may be rejected for quite logical reasons (the editor has just bought a similar piece, he or she ran something too much like it last year), but later queries will benefit from the solid writing of the first as much as by the writer's persistence in breaking into the new market with good writing and good ideas.

Because most freelancers are relative newcomers, this book makes the assumption that a go-ahead or positive reply on speculation, previous item (2), is the most favorable response the writer can consistently expect. When that writer has gained the experience and reputation to move into category (1), payment before or upon delivery, that writer will probably have left the freelance classification in all but a technical sense.

I make a further assumption that is in fact too optimistic: that every editor giving a go-ahead does so with the full intent of ultimately buying the manuscript if, in final form, it meets the promises of the query. Unfortunately, a few editors respond to almost every query by telling the writer to submit the work on speculation. Almost all of those pieces are later rejected. The only tip-off to those editors comes in the type of go-ahead they send. If it is mass-produced or impersonal, beware.

SUBJECT

Again, the purpose of the query letter is to sell first an idea, then a manuscript for publication. The heart of the query letter is that *idea.* Everything else is secondary. The form most likely to sell the idea will dictate the form the letter takes. If the piece is to be solemn in tone, the query should also be solemn. If the topic is fluffy and fun, the letter should show evidence of that same light joy, which is not to say that it should be silly and pointless, but rather that it must enhance the manuscript's consideration—and sale—by showing your ability to write the query as you plan to write the piece.

Too many of my students' query letters fail to show a full grasp of the subject. Often the letters are too short and the facts too sparse or suspect. One way to ensure that the topic is adequately covered is to consider the query letter as a précis or single-page summary of a piece already written, from which the writer must select the "best" order so the editor will know what the piece is about and how it conveys its message. The summary should include the subject and your approach to it, supporting data, the conclusions to be drawn, and the reason a reader should care about the topic in the first place, if that isn't obvious.

EXPERTISE OR PREPARATION

Editors will want to know how you got your facts, whether they are reliable and accurate, and how well you know the field.

This information is particularly important when you write for specialized journals. Editors in the medical field aren't waiting for a piece from a layman who thinks that canker sores may be cured someday. However, they may be interested in cures, methods of treatment, or scientific studies on the causes and treatments of similar viral problems here or abroad. You needn't be a doctor or a scientist. All that editors ask is that you have a firm understanding of the subject and can cite sources and studies that are, as I said, reliable and accurate—and verifiable.

Should you mention your academic background? Only if (1) that background gives you a special, learned insight into the topic, (2) it provides you with a unique sense of the topic, (3) you are writing about academia, or (4) you are writing to academics.

Two editor friends laughed when I asked how they would respond to a list of earned degrees in a query letter. Their replies were the same: "That's fine, but can they write? And can the reader believe what they say?"

PREVIOUS PUBLICATIONS

If you have no previous publications, say nothing. If you have a few and they fall into the church bulletin and hometown newspaper category, once again silence is the best policy—unless that paper serves a major city. Mention previous publications only if they are impressive. If the query letter itself shouts "professional," their absence won't be noted. If the query letter proves that you are a beginner, 100 publications in alphabetical order won't make much difference. They won't be believed.

If I've sold to a publication before, I naturally mention it, particularly if another editor reigned during the earlier sale. Only if I wish to show an editor that I've worked on a wide range of fields when I'm proposing a subject with particularly broad appeal will I give a more extensive list, and then never more than 10 or 12 items.

Beginners are often tempted to puff their credits—to raise a real three to a fictitious 33—by citing magazines they wish they had sold to. A foolish game, really. You will be judged on the manuscript prepared in response to a query go-ahead, and if it shows too little writing skill, not only will the piece be rejected, the editor will wonder how you could have sold so often before. Your name will stick, negatively, and it may well be harder for you to break into print with that editor the next time around. Even worse, what if the editor asks to see specific examples of your previous work?

Sometimes an editor requests tearsheets or samples of earlier published work. An editor occasionally makes the same request after reading a query. Try to find examples as close to the editor's publication as you can, without too much regard to date, although I always include the most recent piece I have in print too. If you have very few sales but examples are asked for, send photocopies of what you do have.

ILLUSTRATIONS

Illustrations include photographs, slides, drawings, maps, charts, and other items used to enhance your manuscript.

Some pieces particularly require illustrations. If you are trying to sell a bloodracer called "How I Caught a 400-Pound *Pirarucú*," you had better have more than one dim slide showing you in an Amazonian setting with a garlike, tongued fish larger than yourself. Likewise, a story about hiking the lost trail across the Andean *páramo* had better come with slides or photos of a trail devoid of Baby Ruth wrappers in a setting convincingly Ecuadorian.

The number of photos and slides you can provide will interest the editor, as will their size and quality. Unless it is germane to the story, who took them is less important than that they were taken. Frequently I am writing in one part of California and trustworthy photographer friends are elsewhere snapping shots for me. A graphics colleague often provides comical drawings to illustrate my humorous pieces, enlarging markets for both of us.

Should you send illustrations with the query letter? I don't because they can get lost en route or go astray at the destination. Mention what you can provide in the query and then wait until the editor requests samples.

With black-and-white photos, I have a proof sheet made instead of prints. I cut out the best shots from the proof and mount them presentably on a regular sheet of paper, like stamps in an album, with double-stick tape or rolled tape on the back. Each shot is numbered, and a caption sheet accompanies each page of these selected proofs explaining the shots by number. If the editor is interested in particular shots, I send the corresponding negatives or a $5 \times 7''$ or an $8 \times 10''$ print, depending on that editor's request or ability to make the prints in-house.

If the editor wants slides, my response is based on

the value of the shots. If I have plenty of slides and the ones requested aren't particularly valuable, I send originals, each with my name and address written on it. A caption sheet accompanies the slides, explaining each.

But if the slides are once-in-a-lifetime shots, I have copies made of the best ones and send the copies in a plastic holder for the editor's selection. The editor indicates which are needed and returns all of the duplicates. Then I send the chosen few—the originals—in the same kind of plastic holder, heavily insured. The system is cumbersome but it works. I've never lost a slide or a client.

———■———

I like a query to outline the article, tell me about how many words the writer intends to supply, how soon the manuscript could be expected, and what illustrative material, if any, is available.

Bill Sonneborn, *former editor*, Michiana Magazine (South Bend Tribune)

CHAPTER 3

A Sample
Query Letter

We have talked around and about query letters. It's time we read one!

The letter that follows (see Query Letter 1 on pages 30–31), as most others in this book, was actually sent to an editor. In almost all of these cases, the letters are precisely as written; in a few instances (mainly cover letters) they are reconstructed from notes when originals were lost or never kept. With one major exception: I have often changed the editors, publications, and addresses and sometimes the names of the people in the letters. The reason is sad but simple: A few readers saw the actual names in the earlier version of this book or in seminar materials and bothered those mentioned!

THE PURPOSE OF THIS QUERY LETTER

It tells editor Allen Hearty that I have information about a person his readers would like to know and that I'd like to write an article about that person.

I could have written a manuscript instead of the

query letter. Hearty would have been able to see how I treated Kurt Gluck, how much copy on fishing was included in the text, and the ratio of dialogue to anecdote and straight narrative. I might even have sent 35mm color slides along so he could see the whole package at once.

It might have taken me 5 to 10 hours to complete some backup research, write the copy (and rewrite and edit the writing), type the final draft, and prepare the slides and captions. All this presumes that I was familiar with *Fishing Today,* had already closely studied the type of material it used, and had a sense of what its readers found interesting.

Instead, the query took 20 minutes to write, perhaps another 20 to rewrite and edit—at most an hour from inception to mailing.

The key point is that Hearty rejected the query, with kind words and encouragement about future ideas. I lost one-fifth to one-tenth the time I would have had I written and sent the manuscript instead of a query. And I wasn't stuck with a written manuscript that would have to be rewritten for the next submission.

Instead, I had a rejection letter and my copy of the query. I lamented the first, then read the second, turned to my list for another market, and had a new query in the mail within 30 minutes. Two weeks later the story was sold! Or at least I had a go-ahead, with some very specific directions about how to slant the biographical piece to interest the second magazine's readers. I wrote it to match those directions and then sold it. Had I just sent the already written manuscript (presuming I had written one for Hearty instead of querying), it would have been rejected again.

The point is obvious. Why write a manuscript when in the same length of time you can write a dozen query letters? When an editor gives you the green light, then you write the article directly for that magazine's readers and for the editor, who knows it is coming and has already penciled it in for a future issue—if it meets the publication's standards.

THERE'S MORE THAN TIME INVOLVED

By penciling in your topic, the editor is involved in the process. He or she has been in your shoes, knows what a writer must do, and is now psychologically part of your doing it. The editor has a vested interest in your manuscript when it arrives. By giving you the go-ahead, by taking your query promise and mentally fitting it into a future issue, the editor has become to a small degree, at least in spirit, your co-author.

Therefore, that editor is far less likely to reject your submission—and far more likely to cheer a job well done! Only two things are guaranteed to turn that spirit against you: sending in something other than what your query promised or submitting a manuscript that is far below professional level.

The point? Reread your query more than once when you write your final manuscript and stick to it! Then make your prose hum. Work, write, edit, move the words around, write again—until your article reads like the best one in the last issue of *Fishing Today*.

Consider the difference between the reception your copy receives and a manuscript some beginner sends in, completely written, unexpected, about a topic new to the editor. Which would Allen Hearty be more likely to buy?

You see, editors expect query letters, not manuscripts. Professionals send queries; amateurs don't—

until they start acting like professionals. By sending queries.

WHY THIS QUERY IS WRITTEN AS IT IS

Fishing Today is a serious magazine little given to humor. It considers fishing less a hobby or restful avocation than a contest between man and all aquatic life. It's proconservation, as that pertains to water and fish, but nonetheless seems intent on showing the reader how to catch the limit every time out. Its one concession: It constantly seeks exciting, new locations for its articles. Its greatest blessing? It pays $1,000 for 1,800 words, and extra for photos! Any wonder why it was first on my market list? The query takes all of these items into consideration.

Subject

The letter has one subject, Kurt Gluck, and one approach, serious and straightforward. The primary link to the magazine is fishing, Kurt's favorite activity. Prominent in the query are types of fish, fishing locales, water, and canoes. The rest of the letter fleshes Kurt out, so we know what he is like and why we should care about him. It also tells why I should write the piece.

Some things aren't said. What is a person with a name like Kurt Gluck doing in Brazil? Where's he from? What's his background? Could he be a Nazi in hiding? (He's not!) There are at least a dozen more questions, but in the limited space of one page they aren't worth answering. Select only those facts that promote your purpose: to sell an idea, and a manuscript, to the editor. You can answer the other questions in the article itself.

Expertise or Preparation

My experience is scarcely mentioned in the *Fishing Today* query. In summary, it says (or implies) that I've been to Brazil recently, attended college there, took photos of Kurt and of fishing on a lake near the Amazon River, and I have information about Gluck.

You didn't notice, I hope, that I know so little about fishing I can't tell which end of the beast bites. Or that I've never actually fished with Gluck. Neither is important, frankly, because if I get the go-ahead from Hearty, I will learn what I need to know and will interview others who have fished with the likable Bavarian.

Remember, be honest but say only what best serves your purpose. If you got the impression that Kurt and I spent weeks harpooning minnows on the tributaries, I'm sorry. That's what good writing can do! Hearty may have guessed, since he said no. But if he had said yes, he would never have known otherwise from the final manuscript. I've raised his expectations and must now live up to them. In print we'd net minnows and harpoon *pirarucús*.

I have four academic degrees centered on Latin America, particularly Brazil, but they aren't mentioned, and are barely referred to, in this query. What would be the purpose?

Previous Publications

Should I list my publications? Should I list 100? Or 200? Why would I? The editor is interested in one thing: Can I give him good copy? I limit myself to noting the number of times I've been in print in magazines at that time. Sometimes I list a few publications similar to the editor's that I am querying to show that I've worked the field. (When writing to *Fishing Today*, of the then 350 items in print not one had been sold to a fishing magazine, so I simply cited the number.)

Illustrations

The half sentence about illustrations in the query could be the difference between a sale or a rejection. It talks about "50 good-to-excellent 35mm slides of Kurt and fishing near Lake Janauari." As often as not with foreign settings, where photos are critical, the editor will ask to see them before giving a go-ahead.

Query Letter 1

> 123 Main Street
> Santa Maria, CA 93456
> (805) 123-4567
> Month 1, Year
>
> Mr. Allen Hearty
> Editor, *Fishing Today*
> 808 Third Street
> New York, NY 10000
>
> Dear Mr. Hearty:
>
> Kurt Gluck is a quiet hero, a soft-spoken legend poking into the Amazon backlands. Never mind that he's the best-known guide from Belém to Iquitos. The other guides think he's crazy.
>
> At 63, he's the last of a vanishing breed of fighters holding off the commercial hacks at the 1,000-mile-inland mecca of Manaus, famous for lost rubber riches and modern-day free port booty. Kurt lives on a back street and is better

known in Tokyo, Munich, and Miami Beach than he is in Brazil.

For $30 a day, for the rich or poor, he will fill his 8-hp outboard motor with gas, point his canoe into the rushing *furos* of the poorly tamed Rio Negro, and enter his beloved wilds. Kurt doesn't hunt, except to survive. He'd rather fish, and few know a greater thrill than to paddle silently at his side in a shaded pool to the curious scrutiny of *cheiro* monkeys and iridescent morpho butterflies, to jolt at the arm-wrenching bite of the fierce *tucunarés*, the clamp-jawed tiger *piranhas*, or even the boat-spilling *pirarucús*, the largest freshwater fish in the world.

Gluck's a tough, gnarled old warrior in love with nature who laughs at stories of man-eating *piranha*, calling them 99% myth. He swims with pink dolphin, pulls teeth, and has put most of his children through medical school.

I've just returned from Brazil, where I went to college some years back. I've been in print in magazines 350 times since then and can provide 50 good-to-excellent 35mm slides of Kurt and fishing near Lake Janauari, an hour from Manaus. Are *Fishing Today* readers ready to share some of this Brazilian adventure and joy, Mr. Hearty?

Gordon Burgett

Let's explore the topic of queries a bit more before reviewing another letter.

WHEN SHOULD YOU QUERY?

Not all writing sales come from query letters, nor do you query for all sales. To help see where querying fits into the selling process, we will use the diagram on page 32 called "The Mechanics of Getting into Print." It is based on our 15-step guide but focuses primarily on the steps taken at and after the query or copy is sent.

Diagram 1 The Mechanics of Getting into Print

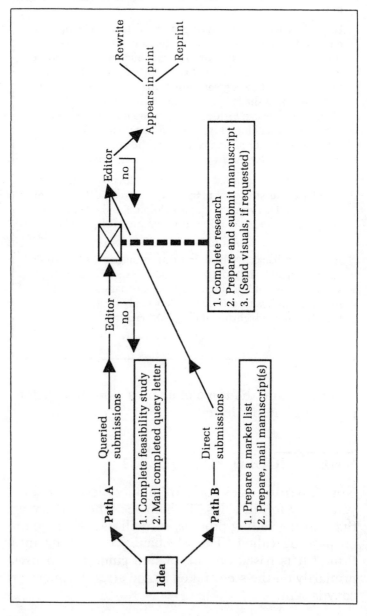

The process begins with an idea and ends with that idea appearing in print, making you rich and renowned. There are hurdles, however, between the idea and the ideal.

Since we explain how query and cover letters follow this process throughout the rest of this book, let's briefly describe the diagram.

Path A is for queried items where the query letter follows the feasibility study. It is mailed to the editor, who responds positively (you complete and submit the copy) or negatively (you query the next editor on your market list). If the editor buys your copy, after responding positively to your query, you appear in print—at least once!

Path B is for direct submissions where, instead of querying, you write and submit the copy from the outset. Again, the editor either accepts or rejects that copy. If it's rejected, send it to another editor (or editors, if simultaneously submitted). If it's bought, *voilá*.

CHAPTER 4

A Second
Query Letter

Let's look at a second actual query letter, with the
original names and all, that is far different in form
and purpose from that lauding Kurt Gluck, and then
follow it, hypothetically, through the steps shown in
Diagram 1.

While devouring a then recent best-seller, I got a
great idea. "Would you be interested in . . . ?" are the
magic querying words, and since the thriller was
called *The Book of Lists*, I wrote the editors asking if
they'd be interested in a list (see Query Letter 2 on
pages 38–39).

Sound balmy, like trying to sell virtue to a paragon?
It would if the Wallace (Wallechinsky) family (father
Irving, son David, daughter Amy) hadn't asked at the
end of the book's foreword for us not to "be listless
. . . (to) join in" and send them lists for the next
edition.

Normally I wouldn't respond to their bid for con-
tributors since I imagine that although they pay for
items used, it isn't much. The time spent hunting for
lists they missed or trying to compile new ones

wouldn't be profitable. I'm not courting penury by intent.

But, I did happen to have two facts stored in a reserve lobe, and they'd take no time at all to develop. I'd written a children's nonfiction article, "The Seven Kings of the Americas," which was a list in itself, plus a fact about one of those kings fit perfectly into another list that *The Book of Lists* contained.

(Some will ask if it is ethical to use the names of the seven kings, and facts about them, again since I had already sold an article in which that appeared. Of course. The magazine didn't buy exclusive rights to the facts, just the copy in which those facts were used. Said in another way, you don't sell ideas, just the specific way in which those ideas are presented.)

So, never one to let unearthed facts get reburied unprofitably, I took 15 minutes to write a query to (1) make the editors aware that the information exists, (2) set up a potential sale, and (3) save me from having to compile an actual list without knowing the preferred format.

I query because if the Wallaces are interested, they will tell me how they want the information sent. Then I can pluck the old facts from my files, type the copy at one sitting, package and mail it, and wait for the check. In the meantime, the idea is out of my mind and in their hands. I am free to do other things, like sending queries to higher-paying markets. If Irving and his kids reply with a "no, thanks," I've lost 15 minutes and a few pennies in stamps. If they want the data, I will reread my copy of the query, match the facts to their directions, and respond promptly.

The system maximizes time-use efficiency and spells success. Enough good ideas well presented will bring you "let-me-see-it" or "go-ahead" replies, and eventually, money in the bank. Your bank.

NOTES ABOUT THE QUERY

A touch of humor as an opener, then a deservedly kind word about *The Book of Lists.* Down to business: I have a potential list and a fact to add to the "9 Most Unusual Monuments in the World" list; they should let me know if they want either prepared for their next edition. The rest of the letter makes the items I can provide more interesting or more desirable.

The query shows that I have read their book and am familiar with the kind of material a follow-up might contain. Also, that I know the material I'm offering for sale well enough to have written about it for print. I suggest a format but leave the choice to them.

There's a minor point worth noting: I haven't mentioned all of the material that I want to sell in the query letter. Six of the seven kings are unnamed; the source of the Dessalines fact isn't cited. I can't prevent the editors from digging up the missing elements, but I can make it a bit harder. One thing is certain, if I didn't write the query at all, I wouldn't have a chance at a sale. And if I don't give enough facts to bring the items to life, then I've also written a letter that will reap no reward. The query, as written, is an attempt to walk that narrow path leading to a pot of gold. The items withheld are token insurance. But most of the query, as with most queries, is done on faith. (The vast majority of publications are honorable. Probably about the same ratio as the writers selling to them.)

Last, there is no reason to mention my publishing credits, though one article in juvenile nonfiction is noted. If the letter reads well, speaks truth with authority, and offers to cite verifiable sources, that should be enough.

Query Letter 2

123 Main Street
Santa Maria, CA 93456
(805) 123-4567
Month 1, Year

Mr. David Wallechinsky
Mr. Irving Wallace
Ms. Amy Wallace
The Book of Lists
P.O. Box 49328
Los Angeles, CA 90046

Dear David, Irving, and Amy:

I bought *The Book of Lists* for the family for Christmas and have scarcely let them see it since! The kids homed in like pigeons to the areas touching on sex. I know because they left fingerprints and food stains before I got there. The entire tome is delightful.

Your readers might enjoy another list I could send you: The Seven Kings of the Americas, the subject of an article I sold to a juvenile magazine. All seven were legitimate rulers of nations we know: three from Haiti, two from Brazil, and two from Mexico. Three were related; three were black, one was mixed, three were from royal European stock. Four were killed in their countries, two died in exile, another died of old age after spending years abroad (part of the time in the United States), deposed. All ruled during the last century. Sources provided, of course.

Would you like the list of the seven prepared in the manner of "10 Unexplored Areas of the World" or "15 Islands for Sale," that is, with the names and some interesting bio data?

Incidentally, the first of the seven kings, Jean-Jacques Dessalines of Haiti, might also be listed in the "9 Most Unusual Monuments in the World" (p. 138), for, like José Olmedo, a statue stands in his honor in a park in Port-au-Prince, Haiti. Mind you, Dessalines not only hated whites, he butchered them with glee. So imagine his chagrin should he discover that the group buying the statue ran out of funds and could find only a secondhand reject from a Central American country of a deposed ruler—who was white!

Please let me know if either the list or the item about Jean-Jacques is worth preparing. Best wishes to all of you.

Gordon Burgett

REPLY TO THE QUERY

A few minutes and a few stamps, two envelopes, and some paper isn't a bad gamble on earning from $25 to several hundred dollars simply to rework some facts that weren't being overused anyway. The reply was cordial but formal: no thanks. I guess I'll just have to wait for somebody else's list book to pop up. Or sell these tidbits as fillers. No gold today.

CHAPTER 5

A Good Query Is Almost Negotiable Tender

Let's set up a hypothetical story and follow it from query to publication. The subject is Lassie.

While pursuing other research, you stumble upon the December 1939 issue of *The Saturday Evening Post*, which contains the first publication of "Lassie Come-Home" by Eric Knight. You probe a bit and find out that the short story was really a book nobody would publish, so in fact Lassie was born, in a literary way, in that issue. Let's go a step further and say that it is seven months short of Lassie's 40th or 50th "birthday." Your idea: to celebrate the gala event by looking back at what the world's most famous dog has been through during that period.

IDEA

You have a salable idea. What you need next is a list of potential markets plus enough support data to make the idea come alive in a query letter.

POSSIBLE MARKETS

One possible market is obvious: the source of the original story, *The Saturday Evening Post*. Other types of magazines that might want to run a family-oriented, pet-based story are general interest, animal, in-flight, women's, children's, and a half-dozen more. So you draw up a list of those fields and then determine an order for querying.

Market Study

To extend our example further, let's say that *Our Family Magazine* appears to be the best market for your idea. It pays handsomely, on acceptance, and runs reams of well-written, general interest–humor–nostalgia copy each month. You head for the library to read the issues for the past three months, paying particular attention to two stories dealing with related topics: a *National Velvet* movie remake, with a look back at the original, and an exposé of Smokey the Bear, fact and fiction. You note the approaches these pieces take, their length, the amount and kind of humor used, and the way that animals are treated.

QUERY LETTER

Then you write a query letter to Ms. Leona Stokes, the managing editor, explaining your idea. Bring it to life, include your writing background, and add suggestions about illustrations.

Interesting facts about Lassie can be found in the library listings under movies, radio (yes, Lassie was a radio star, barking and growling over the airwaves on command), TV, and famous animals/pets. You tell Ms.

Stokes that the first Lassie in the movies was really "Pal," a male so full of thistles and burrs when he came to audition he was literally a sore sight. That collies had been avoided in American movies because they were thought to be too nervous in front of a camera. That "Pal" had been so hard to control as a puppy, his owner actually paid Rudd Weatherwax, "Lassie's" trainer, to keep him. That when the collie kissed Roddy McDowall, in *Lassie Come Home,* after bounding across a schoolyard in a scene that brought tears to the eyes of a war-worn America, he was actually licking ice cream off the boy's face. That the story itself was told to Knight when he was a boy growing up in Yorkshire, England, by an uncle who claimed that it was true, and that come-home dogs were reputedly common in that area, trained to come home the night after they were sold, to be resold again! Finally, that Eric Knight never saw the 1943 movie. He was killed in the war before it was released.

These facts are artfully woven into the query letter for one reason: to convince Leona Stokes that her readers will find the full piece as tantalizing as the excerpts she has just read.

You write the letter, fold it, insert it into a large envelope with another, smaller, self-addressed and stamped envelope (SASE), and mail the lot to *Our Family Magazine.* Then you wait, patiently.

"GO-AHEAD" REPLY

Let's imagine that Ms. Stokes is delighted with the idea and thinks it will fit in the coming December issue, with a cover in honor of the anniversary. But she doesn't know you or your work. She replies, tempering her enthusiasm and noting that if the piece can be in her hands within a month, she will gladly consider it on speculation. A go-ahead letter!

DILEMMA

A dilemma! The research and writing will take considerable time. If she rejects the final manuscript, you'll have to redo it to fit some other magazine's needs. Should you go ahead on the chance that she'll buy it or keep querying until you get a firm guarantee of purchase before investing the time?

Be realistic. Who is going to pay you $500, or even $100, to write something for them when they don't even know if you are literate? Granted, you wrote a captivating query, but who (besides me) publishes query letters? And how does the editor really know that you wrote the query letter at all, that you won't just take the cash and dash, or, even if you have the most honorable of intentions (an assumption not always made about writers), you will be able to provide copy that is printable?

In my own case, I look upon speculation replies, like Ms. Stokes', as money all but in hand. Since I began using queries I've sold from 85 to 90% of the pieces submitted on speculation—and the rest, with two exceptions, to other buyers.

Can you reasonably expect Leona Stokes or any editor to wire you a purse of doubloons just because you promise her a Pulitzer prize piece? Hardly. Would you if you were the editor? First you must submit copy as good as or better than that promised in the query letter. Presume that Ms. Stokes penciled the item on her December calendar when you were given the go-ahead. Your chances of appearing in that issue are better than 50-50—unless you ruin them. Even if the copy isn't usable as sent, there is the possibility that she will suggest ways to improve it, so you can try again with a rewrite. (Even if the answer is no, you can still sell it to other markets on your market list.)

WRITE THE REPLY

Therefore, if you get a go-ahead on speculation, stir that library dust, pound the keys, and whip up a first-class article. Think beyond that first sale. The next time you confront Ms. Stokes with a blue-ribbon idea in a well-written query you won't be an unknown, and she just might send you that $500 in advance. Even if she doesn't (and most editors never do), each future go-ahead will be closer to a sure sale, as long as you consistently send copy that matches what you promise in your query and that is as well-written as the other articles in the publication.

YOU'RE IN PRINT

Say that you do churn out several thousand words bringing the many Lassies back to full, tail-wagging life. The editor likes your piece, sends a check, and about November you receive from one to five copies of the coming issue of *Our Family Magazine.* You're in print!

Sound too simple? There's no magic to selling your writing. Perhaps 8 of 10 sales follow that pattern. The highest hurdle comes not in selling a queried manuscript but in finding a publication willing to look at your idea. Still, if the idea has public appeal, if your queries are specifically tailored to the respective publications, if those publications sell to the readers most interested in your idea, and if your letter shows by its content and form that you are a capable writer, most ideas you set forth for print can result in a paycheck.

... OR YOU'RE REJECTED

Let's throw some curves into the setup, as examples of how queries are still the best use of time and energy. Let's say that Leona Stokes hates collies, is up to her nostrils in nostalgia, and has an odious father-in-law with the same first name as yours. For some mysterious reason she rejects your query.

Disappointing, but not fatal. Go to the next magazine on your list, read it, tailor a query to its needs, then wait again. Ms. Lulu Potts, editor-in-chief, waxes ecstatic in her reply. "It's wonderful, I'm so excited . . ." So you conjure up a manuscript that is properly "wonderful" and send it to her. She rejects it flat! "I've changed my mind," she says, and that is that.

You have a number of responses. You can fire off a scalding reply questioning whether she has a mind to change. That will fail to get the piece bought, and it may close her market to you forever.

You can kick Lassie in the penside and forget the whole thing, which also won't feed the chickens.

You can reread your copy of the query letter and see how your manuscript differs from what you led Lulu to expect. Or see if it is so far below publishable quality that any editor would reject it, however wide-eyed he or she was at the outset. In either case, you must make corrections the next time around. If the manuscript is solid but not what the query paints, change brushes and paint a truer likeness in the next query. If the manuscript is poorly done, do it the second time as you should have the first.

The reality is that you still have a manuscript in your hands. What should you do with it? You can either query the next market on the list or send it with a cover letter (not mentioning that others found it unusable!) to that same market.

We've been too hard on Ms. Potts! Let's imagine that she responded positively to the manuscript and was no less delighted with the final version than she was excited by your query. Except for one thing: You spent all of your time writing about oddities, like history and fame, and she really wanted a piece about Lassie's grooming. "Will you please rewrite the article making that the main focus, with examples?"

In other words, no sale unless you invest more time in research and writing. Free time.

If you know where to find the information that she wants and the alterations will be fast and minor, grumble to yourself, do the rewrite, and be sure to ask for more specific guidelines from Ms. Potts *before* preparing another piece for her magazine.

If she is really asking for a totally different manuscript, that's not nearly so bad. Set aside the gem she has rejected (to sell elsewhere) and write the last word on collie grooming for Lulu, accepting her check with both grace and haste. Then sell the manuscript you set aside to another editor, either through another query or by submitting the manuscript, directly by mail, with a cover letter.

There is no end to the imaginary pitfalls that can be invented to confuse and frighten you. But why? Most new writers do enough of that inventing themselves. Once you find an interested buyer, it is rare that the piece won't be bought if it lives up to the expectations you created in the query letter.

Later we will discuss simultaneous queries, reprints, second rights, and overseas sales. Those are the areas where exquisite complications most often occur.

CHAPTER 6

It Starts with an Idea

You can think up the most exciting idea in the world, but if others won't read past the first sentence, your idea will suffer a silent, unprinted commercial death.

The crassness of that truth disturbs many new writers, often fresh from the less competitive pastures of academia, where everything written is read and matched to a grade. In the commercial world, though, nothing forces anyone to read what you write, much less pay to buy the publication it's in. And if no one will read it or buy the publication, you won't get rich by writing nonfiction. You won't even get poor.

So that is the test that must be applied to every idea before it is framed in a query: Will it be bought and read if it gets in print?

The editor knows what his or her readers will buy, and that determines what he or she will buy from you.

I once researched a potential article about the circumflex in Portuguese, an odd-looking hatlike symbol (^) that occasionally appears atop the letters *a*, *e*, and *o*. This curious relic has a noble and intriguing history, first seen in Greek before changing form and use in other tongues. Still, I couldn't find more than a handful of philologists and Lusophiles who could even pronounce the word, much less want to read about it. The topic was doomed. It never got to the querying stage.

On the other hand, the Lassie story has been the object of at least 50 queries, has appeared in print 20-plus times, and almost appeared as a book about how pets find their way home over long distances. The idea has a huge market: a nation of dog lovers from 6 to 60 who grew up with the tricolored collie. They remember the movies and TV series and want to read about how they and America's best-known dog have aged together.

Still, it's not enough to have an idea to write a query. A thinking writer can churn out 50 ideas an hour. Most of them don't merit querying because their scope is too narrow or shallow, they have recently been written about, they are outdated, or they are too dull. The ones that survive are those with some built-in appeal to a sizable portion of the reading, paying public.

IDEAS THAT SELL

New writers think that to sell they must have a unique, original, or singular idea. Actually, ideas that sell are usually the reverse: They concern the things that affect you and me every day. They disturb, amuse, irk, or inspire us. How will we get around when gas hits $4 a gallon? Will another Messiah appear in our lifetime, and will we recognize Him/Her? When will there be a vaccine against cancer? How can I keep going when it all seems so hopeless? Why can't kids read or write? How can I get more sex, happiness, money, love, friends, security, appreciation, joy, satis-faction—one, any, or all!

If you think of an idea annually, it may not be salable. If you think of it weekly, you may have some-thing. If you think of it daily, zero in. (If you think of it five times a day, you have an obsession!)

STUDY YOUR MARKETS

What do readers want to know about? Pick a publica-tion in which you'd like to see your material pub-lished. Study its table of contents for the past six months. Reduce each article to the topic it discusses. Those are the subjects its readers pay to explore. Take those words and move on. Ask new questions about those topics. Focus on one that particularly interests you. Research it, query, write the manuscript, and when you see yourself on those pages, you'll wonder why it all seemed so hard before.

Don't shy away from a subject because it has been in print often. When many think of travel, they think of Hawaii, Rio de Janeiro, Hong Kong, Paris, Switzer-land, Santa Maria, Ireland, or perhaps Nova Scotia. Take any of those places and see what working ques-tions about them served as the core for articles. Look up articles in the *Reader's Guide to Periodical Liter-ature* for the past two years. List those questions. Then ask six more. One or many salable query ideas will be hiding in the new six.

TIMING

Timing is crucial. That means getting a good topic into print before others do. To make sure that an identical idea hasn't just been printed, check the

Reader's Guide, the contents of the magazines most likely to have run an article about the topic, major newspaper indexes, and book titles in the subject listings of your library.

There's another aspect to timing. Nothing angers an editor like a query with a dynamite idea that must be used immediately—or sooner. Remember, the query is to be written by a professional for professional consideration. Pros know that magazines have fairly long lead times. Monthlies often need copy and illustrations three to four months in advance. Sunday supplements are often finalized six weeks or longer before publication, and even daily newspapers can take up to a week to work in copy. The moral is plain: Plan ahead—way ahead.

If you are hoping to write about the Boston Marathon in April, query in August or September. Holiday issues need even more time. Query a year in advance or your idea may be held from print for two years! With your luck that editor probably pays on publication!

FIT YOUR IDEA THROUGH AN HOURGLASS

It helps if you can visualize where the query letter, an idea, and you are in relation to the publication. Think of an hourglass on its side. You are on one end and the publication is on the other. At the narrow passageway sits the editor.

You must take an idea and reduce it in scope to fit through the opening. Let's say that you want to write about baseball for a major sports magazine. Great! It needs stories about baseball. But the whole topic is too large to squeeze through, so you must pick a particular aspect of baseball, an angle or item or way of seeing facts that will excite readers and at least interest the editor.

You decide to focus on baseball in Brazil, especially among Japanese Brazilians living in the São Paulo area.

Now you must present your idea in a query letter that will gain the editor's approval. Sometimes, even though the new topic will fit through, the editor won't let it. The bald fact is that editors can stop any idea you try to pass through the funnel. On the other hand, they need good ideas, and to survive as editors they must let enough get through to fill their pages each week or month.

The analogy may be a bit simplistic, but it accurately puts our parts into a proper relationship. An even simpler, or more simplistic, example would have the editor behind a door you must go through to appear in the magazine. The door opens only when you say the right words in an acceptable way. The words are framed in the query.

———■———

Many of our rejections occur because authors want to write on the same old subjects. If we bought all the articles we're offered on hummingbirds entitled "Nature's Little Helicopters," we could fill several issues a year with them.

> *Claire Miller, managing editor,* Ranger Rick Magazine *(National Wildlife Federation)*

CHAPTER 7

When Should You Send the Manuscript?

When you get a go-ahead from a query, the editor giving you the nod is high in your concerns. Unfortunately, you are far less important to that editor, who has a dozen articles in process plus other editorial worries, like reading query letters to find more ideas for future copy. The editor will remember your idea, maybe your name, but likely little more.

For that reason, I query only when I think I can get the manuscript to the editor within a three-week period. That way, from the date I get the green light until the "package" is en route, there is a sufficiently short period of time for the editor to have it and me in mind, and, should it require some rewrite, there is still time to make alterations before publication.

Furthermore, I often state in the query that the manuscript and attachments will be in the editor's hands within three weeks.

There is one major exception. When travel is required, I query as much as six months in advance, telling the editor when I plan to leave and return. To the return date I add about three weeks and promise to have the copy in the editor's hands by that date.

I've tried to convince the editor that I am a professional, at least by the content and appearance of my query, and that same professionalism must extend to honoring time commitments. Thus I do everything possible to get the copy in the editor's hands within 21 days.

Yes, I have missed deadlines, but rarely. In each case, before the third week, I wrote or called the editor explaining why a delay would take place and when the copy would arrive—within 10 days, maximum, of the earlier deadline.

I've had editors tell me that they like receiving the copy so quickly. It gives them a chance to see the material while the idea is still hot. I think it results in many more sales, though there is no way to prove that. It also forces me to get to the writing quickly and to do a more thorough prequery job of researching and annotating sources.

CHAPTER 8

Research Before Writing

A query letter saves you time. It lets you delay most of the research, the interviews, and the bulk of your writing until you have a specific readership to write for and a near-promise that your work will be published and you will be paid.

How much time should you spend researching your topic before writing a query? My answer is about as precise as Abraham Lincoln's when he was asked how long a man's legs should be: "Long enough to touch the ground."

The same holds true, figuratively, for a query. You need to research your query until it is accurate and impressive and you know that you can deliver the manuscript it promises.

Suppose that it's getting close to the year 2000, the bimillennium A.D. Since it's at least a once-in-a-life-time event, clever writers will be nudging each other to cover it in print.

The question is how you approach it. You might decide to focus on the first millennium A.D. to show how much has happened since that time. Off to the library—to slim pickings. Oh yes, Otto III beheaded Pope John XVI and designated his own tutor as Pope Sylvester II that year. The Moslems ruled what is now Spain, and Ethelred the Unready had his hands full with the Vikings in England, until Sven I, King of Denmark, sent him packing to Normandy. The Magna Carta was yet to be signed and the Crusades were further off yet. Eric the Red had gone from Iceland to Greenland only 19 years earlier. The New World Indians didn't know they were, and they still had only one another to contend with.

Not all that interesting, frankly.

So you decide to see how much things have changed in just the last 100 years in the United States. Bingo: 1900 was a whole lot different. Better yet, it was a bumper year for interesting, ironic, and humorous events, well-peopled with characters whose names are still known today. You decide that a fast, fun, tightly woven string of happenings, names, anecdotes, and ironies will be your format. What do you do next?

FIND A MARKET

Find markets ripe for such fun, then focus on one, identify its readers, and pluck from your pool of materials appropriate tales, events, names, and facts to make your query sparkle, as a sample of the merriment and insight readers can expect in the final copy.

LIBRARY RESEARCH

You will need a firm understanding of what happened in 1900. That requires reliable sources at hand—great starters like the Time-Life *This Fabulous Century* series or the superb Trager chronology. You can flesh out the day-by-day events through microfilm copies of the *New York Times* and other newspapers. Check the biographies of Robert Peary, Leonard Wood, William Randolph Hearst, William Jennings Bryan, J. P. Morgan, and Booker T. Washington. What did people buy? Get a copy of the Sears Roebuck "wish book," the catalogue.

What do you find? A new baseball league, the American. Gibson girls. *McGuffey's Reader.* William McKinley a year from an assassin's bullet; Teddy Roosevelt a year from the White House and the Square Deal. Eggs for 12 cents a dozen; wallpaper a nickel a roll. Eight thousand registered cars, no trucks or buses. And 115 lynchings. The Civil War 35 years past; the war with Spain just finished. Life expectancy of 47.3 years, wages at 22 cents an hour, with 59 hours an average work week. The fastest speed ever traveled, 65.79 miles per hour. The newest household gadgets were telephones (17.6 per 1,000), typewriters, and sewing machines. A cornucopia of fun facts, just as starters.

From those sources (and their sources, gleaned from their footnotes and bibliographies) you select the proper choice of items for the query and final manuscript, using the interests of your potential readers as a gauge. You also find a way to relate the year 1900 to the bimillennium, to show the editor why he or she should even be interested in looking back 100 years rather than concentrating solely on the present.

QUERY

Armed with the material necessary to bring your query to life, to substantiate the claims made in it, and to justify the editor's picking 1900 instead of the year 1000 or 2000, you need research no further at this point. Write the query, note the sources for your own use later, and go on to something else. If you receive a go-ahead, reactivate the sources, find more, organize the manuscript, write it, fill in the gaps with additional research, double-check the facts elsewhere, edit the opus, and send it off, keeping some form of source identification in your final rough copy to substantiate any item challenged later. Tell the editor in a cover note that you can cite the sources of all points made in the text.

INTERVIEWING

Interviewing is another form of research. If your piece requires comments or quotes from living sources, make certain that you can speak with them when needed. If they are readily accessible, contact them before writing the query, explaining what you have in mind and asking them a key question or two, to work their replies into the query. Should they agree to give you a longer interview later, that's all you need. Others may have to be contacted through their agents or friends. Whatever method you use, be certain they will be available and will be able to provide you with the type of information you are promising the editor.

In summary, most queries require some research. Do as much as you need to write an accurate, exciting query. Then read closely what you have written to make certain you can provide proof of every point made or implied and that you will be able to add the necessary facts, quotes, and other items promised in the query. When that is done, so are you, until you are told to send the manuscript.

CHAPTER 9

Then Write to the Editor As You Would Write to a Human Being

What is an editor? A human, probably male, 35–55, harried, hairless, something like an underpaid neighbor. He's cynical, his eyes burn, and the day he gets your query will be the day his half-spaced kid tries to drive a 1979 Dodge through a tree. Oh yes, he's also the person you must convince, in a one-page letter, that you should be paid to write for his publication.

Lately, he's just as likely to be a she, with all the above but more hair.

In either case, not only has the editor never met you, but probably never will, nor want to unless you and your prose bring the publication more readers.

If editors loved their mail and cherished the moments when they could close their doors, read leisurely, chuckle appropriately, and ponder often, that would be one thing. But most editors treat their mail as though it's radioactive, postponing its painful perusal until the next Ice Age, or at least until Thursday, late.

What depresses them is the quality of the letters and the impossibility of using all the good ideas that the better ones contain. Imagine having to choose from 100 to 2,000 queries a month the best 6 or 16 that will see print. Rejecting so many ideas would be far worse if so many of the letter writers didn't eliminate themselves by writing abysmally or saying nothing worth consideration.

To qualify you for writing one of those chosen articles, your query must shine like a gem in a bed of pebbles.

READ THIS TWICE

Your letter will shine only if it convinces the editor that your idea—and the treatment you are going to give it—is so special, so interesting, so vital to readers that it would be foolish not to respond at once urging that your manuscript be sent Air Mail Special Delivery.

Remember those words. They are the heart of selling and querying. If the subject of your query isn't so special, so interesting, so vital, it will probably earn a rejection. Yet if you simply say that it is, in so many words, you've also failed to do what a selling writer must: Convey those verities by the tone and content of the query itself.

If the first paragraph of your letter doesn't make the editor want to know what's in the second paragraph, your letter won't work. If that editor has any doubts about the idea you are selling, the letter isn't clear. If the editor doesn't respond quickly, or at least set it aside to act on later (or send it to others on the staff for their thoughts), you've wasted your energy. The way to keep your letter out of the rejection pile is to present a salable topic factually, excitingly, and articulately.

Having said that, I can also say that every selling writer can cite a query that missed on almost every point but still resulted in a sale.

Ignore those exceptions in the beginning. Stick with moneymaking eye-openers that will stand out in the editor's mind. Not only do you want the editor to set your letter aside, you want him or her to picture the final manuscript in print, with illustrations, and then write the topic on the calendar for use in a particular future issue. When the editor replies, giving you a go-ahead and perhaps suggesting a length, deadline, and amount to be paid upon acceptance, you want that editor to be waiting for the finished product with the same eager anticipation with which you waited for his or her reply.

The ideal query letter should convey the feeling that you and the editor are in a joint venture to delight the readers of the publication so they will show your article to their friends, who will immediately send for subscriptions so they don't miss your next appearance on those pages.

YOU ARE YOUR QUERY LETTER

Remember, all an editor knows about you is what he or she can read on one sheet of paper—your letter. If the letter is written on spotted butcher paper, what does that say? If it contains three mispelled [sic] words in the first paragraph, does it show a solid command of written English? If the query is duller than wet cotton yet promises an exciting article, which should be believed, the promise or the proof?

Alas, editors are about as human as we are, and they like others to succeed, especially when that success adds to their own. Give them something that will help them produce better magazines and all will prosper. Gain their confidence with solid query letters, and then make good on the gain with copy as good or better than that promised. That's a formula certain to tame and win any editor.

———■———

Appropriate query letters make an editor's job much easier, and enlightened self-interest is a powerful motivation.

Susan Carr Jenkins, former
executive editor, Medical
Times

CHAPTER 10

To Which Editor Should You Write?

The best way to find out to whom the query letter should be sent is to check the current *Writer's Market*. If it says "send all queries to Mr. J. Johnson, Managing Editor," the only remaining question is whether he still holds that position. Check the most recent issue of the publication, and then send your query to Johnson or the current managing editor.

If the *Writer's Market* listing doesn't indicate a person or position, try the managing editor or the section editor where your idea would most likely appear. The larger the publication, the less likely it is that you should write directly to the editor-in-chief, or the equivalent. More often, the managing editor or section editor weeds through queries, pulls the most promising, works them into idea possibilities for coming issues, and takes those workups to the editor-in-chief for discussion and/or approval, replying to you after a decision has been made.

If the publication doesn't appear in the *Writer's Market*, it means either that it has folded (and definitely isn't the place to query) or, simply, it isn't listed. Check first to see if it is still sold on a regular basis, and, if so, find the list of editors (usually near the table of contents), the address, and other related information.

QUERY A CURRENT EDITOR

Is it really that important to send your query to a current editor? Consider a talk I had with the managing editor of a sports magazine that had refilled this position three times in 30 months. He had a rule of thumb in replying to queries or manuscripts that he felt was typical, in principle, of other editors he knew. If queries or manuscripts were addressed to the first editor, who had been gone more than two years, they were kept in a box for some weeks, unopened, and finally inserted in their own SASEs, along with a rejection note, and the material was returned unread. If there was no SASE, it was dumped.

If the previous editor's name was used, the queries were read as they arrived since that person had departed only six months back, but the manuscripts—which the magazine did not want without a previous query—were returned, unread, in about two weeks.

Any query sent to the current editor was read the day it arrived and acted upon promptly. His logic was simple: If the person hadn't read the publication for two years, which was implied by the use of the first editor's name, the writer had no idea of the substantial changes the magazine had undergone. Even the use of the previous editor's name indicated that the writer was violating a common-sense requirement for professionals, that they keep current on publications and their top staff. Using the wrong name meant that it had been at least six months since the writer had checked the publication. Even if the writer had flipped through a more recent copy, he or she hadn't had enough sense to look up the name of the current editor.

Calling the editor by the wrong name isn't the brightest way to win favor. Petty? Perhaps, but the editors hold all the chips.

CHAPTER 11

When You Don't Need Query or Cover Letters

At the outset, ask one basic question about each item: "Should it be queried before it is written?" That question raises four follow-up questions about how to send the item to the editor:

1. Should it be submitted, after being queried and receiving a go-ahead, without an accompanying cover letter?
2. Should it be submitted, after being queried and receiving a go-ahead, with an accompanying cover letter?
3. Should it be submitted without a query but with a cover letter?
4. Should it be submitted without either a query or a cover letter?

Let's address ourselves to the basic question plus follow-ups (1) and (4) here, leaving the elements involving the use of cover letters until later.

What should be queried? Nonfiction articles. Plus

humorous articles (where the topic is queried and the humor is the style of the writing, not the sole purpose of the piece) and nonfiction books, soon to be explained. Syndicated and overseas items fall into a gray area where either queries or cover letters can be appropriate, so they too will receive special discussion later.

There is no reason to send a cover letter with any of these queried items if the copy and support material (photos, captions, diagrams) are sent promptly or when promised, unless there is something new or additional the editor must know. More on that when we discuss cover letters.

When should material be sent directly, without a query or a cover letter?

GREETING CARDS

By the time you write a query, you could have typed most of the studio lines, mottoes, plaque sayings, or whatever it is you want to sell. And what would you say anyway? "Do you want to buy some funny greeting card lines?" Of course they do; that's why they're in the business. But how does anyone know that yours are funny, and usable, without seeing them? The same goes for card poetry, slogans, buttons, and almost anything else these publishers buy, with the exception of book or booklet ideas and new product formats, where a query should accompany an example of what you have in mind.

FILLERS

These work as a unit and are, as the name implies, copy used to fill extra space, often "ad holes." Most are 1,000 words or less, some as short as a joke or quip. For the editor to see whether the item works, whether it holds together and provides the type of message needed to fill a space, the editor must see the item complete and finished. Many fillers rely on humor, which makes it doubly important to send them directly, so the editor can see if they are funny. (Incidentally, you can submit more than one filler at the same time. Each, of course, must be a complete and different unit.) If some special commentary is needed, that should be sent in a cover letter with the copy.

HUMOR

How can you convince an editor that a humorous piece is funny in a query letter? The query may have him or her gasping for air between guffaws, but the actual piece may be flatter than the last Neanderthal. So save your stamps and typing finger and just send the copy itself. One thing more: A humorous piece relies almost solely on its humor to be bought, like the zanies in *Mad Magazine.* If you are writing a regular article from a humorous slant, where the information is more important than the humor, call it "humorous" and query as you would with a general interest item. Again, only if additional information, which would enhance the item's sale, must be shared with the editor should you send a cover letter with the text.

FICTION

If an editor can't tell if the humor is funny enough through a query letter, even less can he or she tell whether the components of good fiction—characters, plot, dialogue, setting—work together just because you swear, on your mama's reputation, that they do. Let the editor read the fiction. For short stories, send in the entire work. For novels, see what the publisher has said in *Writer's Market* about how material should be submitted, and then send a synopsis and key chapters, or the whole manuscript, as indicated. Your mother will thank you.

The following topics are discussed later in the chapters about cover letters: simultaneous submissions, reprints, direct submissions (including fillers and fiction), photos/illustrations, syndication, overseas sales, and delayed submissions.

CHAPTER 12

What a Good Query Letter Looks Like

A query letter is a business letter, not a chatty, informal how's-the-family exchange between old friends, even if the editor, by chance, also happens to be an old friend. You are asking for money in exchange for a service. You want to be paid for researching, writing, and permitting the use of your labors.

So the appropriate form for such a transaction is that of a business letter: concise, direct, functional. The examples in this book show one form of business letter. Consult your library for books describing and showing other forms.

Query letters should be single-spaced so they can be read faster and the message can be contained, if possible, on one page. They should be neat, error-free (the use of correction fluid or filler is acceptable if the final result is easy to read), and written on white paper, unless one consistently uses a very light gray, cream, or pastel. Flaming red, white, and blue paper or white type on black paper, for example, shouts "showboat" and creates doubt in the editor's mind about your seriousness, maturity, or perhaps even sanity.

Put in another light, let's suppose you ran an ad asking for all qualified writers interested in preparing your biography to appear at a certain address at a stated time and three showed up. Without knowing more than you could see (like an editor with a query letter in hand), would you be most likely to hire (1) a person neat in appearance, clean, and dressed in conventional form, (2) a person with dashes of mud artlessly scattered about his face and clothing, with a tear in one shoe and a price tag hanging from one sleeve, or (3) a person wearing a three-foot-tall hat with pigeon feathers poking from it, a blazing violet neck wrap that partially obscured his face and most of his torso, and electric yellow-blue high-heeled shoes?

A conventional business letter is analogous to (1). In form, not too exciting, but not too alarming either. No distractions delay or obstruct consideration of the writer's message. The second person may be like an error-filled, slapdash letter. If its writer thinks so little of the letter's appearance, can that writer be trusted to do a thorough job researching an article? Will the final manuscript show adherence to accuracy? Maybe, but the editor has to overcome serious misgivings created by the letter's first impression.

The third letter is akin to the third person: a screaming missive on scarlet paper typed with green ribbon, smelling of perfume (or is it rum?), and spiced with such starred and underlined "grabbers" as **reply instantly, chance-of-a-lifetime, I'm your person,** etc. It shouts so many hair-raising messages that an editor, whose reputation and scalp depend on the writer's output, can't help but have grave doubts.

The point is simple: Let the body of the letter sell both your idea and you as the person who should write about it. The form of the letter should be so secondary and so supportive that nothing delays the reader from leaping into the written message. Neither errors nor strikeovers, hand-scribbled footnotes, eye-yanking arrows, gaudy paper, or off-color ribbons should pull the reader's attention from the letter's crucial contents. Everything in the letter, stated and implied, should work in your favor. Its form should say that you are a person who is serious about writing, attentive to detail, careful, businesslike, mature, and able to write well.

The editor, in most cases, has no idea who you are, if you are 9 or 90, sowing your oats or going to seed, fat or flat, Ivy League or bush league, active or radioactive. And he or she probably doesn't care. What the editor wants is a professional writer who will produce an article that will sell more copies of that editor's publication, that is accurate, well-written, and submitted before or when it is due. Your letter must reinforce your professional image.

All the editor knows about you at the first contact is what he or she can see and read in the query letter. That is the sum total of the clues the editor must decipher in deciding whether to give you a go-ahead. If the written message of that query is extraordinarily convincing, detracting visuals in the letter's form and appearance may be overlooked. But if there are enough clues that the writer isn't professional, at least in intent, doubts will surface. Too many doubts and the query will end up in the reject pile, even though the idea posed may be very good.

———■———

Make sure your spelling, grammar, and punctuation are perfect. A well-written letter is the best writing sample you can present. A letter that is sloppily written or haphazardly typed (always type a query letter) will indicate to the editor that the manuscript would be just as sloppy and possibly inaccurate.

Susan Carr Jenkins, former executive editor, Medical Times

CHAPTER 13

What a Query Letter Doesn't Say

A query letter should be positive. Tell the editor the idea you wish to develop, what tools and special skills you bring to the task, information about your past writing experience, and so on. The rest remains unsaid. It's hard enough to sell an idea in a good query letter without saying too much and creating doubt.

PREVIOUS PUBLICATIONS

For example, do you mention that you've never, or seldom, been in print before? Do you attempt to overwhelm the editor with your honesty and frankness, hoping to woo that lucky soul into giving you your first big break by laying your record bare? I wouldn't. Nor would I lie and invent publications or an impressive number of items supposedly sold. I wouldn't say a word. Rather, I'd let a tight, fast, professional sounding query letter say it all by implication: This idea is from a writer able and eager to produce good copy needed by your publication (whether or not that writer has sold before). Don't mention previous publications unless they are impressive. Write so well that the editor is thinking about how to get you to write for the magazine again and again. Think big by making this query special.

NAME CHANGE

If you're a woman and want to write for a men's magazine, or the reverse, a man writing for the women's pages, just go to it, but consider using only your initials instead of your name. Appear as B. R. Hawkins in a hockey story for *Boys Will Be Boys*, rather than as Bobbie Rae. Unless the sex switch is important to the piece—"I Was the First Lady Boxer in Latvia"—I'd write the query, give initials or a name in keeping with the topic, produce first-class copy, and cash the check.

MONEY

Should you ask about money in the query? If you've been writing for a while, you will gain a feel for this kind of thing and will know your steady buyers and their ways, as well as their pay ranges. But newcomers are best advised to keep cash out of the query. Save that for later, if necessary—at least until the editor responds with a go-ahead. In a response the editor frequently indicates an amount, plus information about length, deadline, and sometimes slant.

If your costs are going to be greater than the payment, you have some choices: Adjust the costs or haggle, lovingly, to get the publication to help with or totally pay your expenses. Most magazines won't pay travel for new writers, and many won't pay expenses for any kind of speculation (not assigned) go-aheads. (Or use the material in other ways in other articles.) Just save the haggling until after you have a positive reply, when the editor is at least committed to looking at the copy with intent to use it.

Writer's Market lists payment rates so you should have at least an idea at the outset about the amount you can expect. First-time purchases generally stick close to the listed rates; a modest increase can be expected for later purchases.

KNOWLEDGE OF THE SUBJECT

If you have an uplifting desire to write a piece about ballooning and sail off a query on the subject, don't confide in the editor that you "know nothing about ballooning but will learn through research." If the editor's lukewarm about the subject anyway, that interest will float away. Or if the subject strikes the editor's fancy, you'll be passed over for somebody better informed. Your obligation is to learn about the topic *before* querying so that the slant suggested and the support material mentioned will be accurate, and the article proposed can be written. Then if you get a go-ahead and you learn about ballooning while completing your research, that is your business. The editor's interest is in a solid, reliable article about ballooning, not how and when your knowledge was gained.

Writers needn't be experts on every subject they cover. Yet to query with no knowledge and to expect an editor to pay you to learn the basic facts later is to underestimate the seriousness of professional writing.

Study the subject well before firing off your query, because if you don't, the time will come when you will be unable to find 200 words to back up the best made promise of 2,000, and that will cost you an article and a client. Forty-five minutes in a library or talking with an expert will save you much time and shame. Which backs us into another problem: a promise for an article that nobody can write.

UNWRITABLE TOPICS

No sane editor (which includes most) believes that the Empire State Building is made of snow or that Superman really lived. Yet there is a huge playing field between what everybody knows and what nobody will believe, and freelancers often find themselves skirting its edges.

If you propose writing an article proving that popcorn causes sterility, you had better have scientifically acceptable proof and sterile examples before you even think about a query. If you want to prove that dogs find their way home over long distances by reading maps, the same thing applies. You'd better have a kennel of dogs, or at least a few, who can find a freeway exit using a road map—plus an explanation of how this alarming ability works—before you dust off your typewriter and start twisting the editor's tail.

The key word here is *substantiation*. Without it,

that playing field can turn into a graveyard for aspir-
ing but unprepared beginners.

———■———

*We want our query writers to explain why we
can trust their facts: Are they experts, do they
have firsthand knowledge, or can they at least
cite reliable references?*

> *Claire Miller, managing
> editor,* Ranger Rick
> Magazine *(National
> Wildlife Federation)*

CHAPTER 14

What You Can Expect Back When

E very good query deserves a response. The question is what kind of response and when.

Market listings usually indicate response times, which generally vary from a week to many months. Those times refer to manuscripts. Queries, from my experience, are answered sooner, within a week to 10 days on an average. Even when an editor dallies, the delay is seldom as long as that indicated in the *Writer's Market*.

The type of response you can expect is very much related to the type and quality of query letter sent. A well-written, thorough, exciting query almost always gets a personal reply from an editor, whether that editor is interested or not. Even rejections to such queries often include an invitation to query again. That is logical, since a well-done query tells an editor that this is a professional writer who may later have something valuable to offer.

REJECTIONS

To a good query, an editor will often say why the idea can't be considered at present: a similar piece is in hand or en route, it is too close to something recently used, the idea sits too far to the side of the readers' interests, the setting is outside the publication's main circulation, and so on. The editor may suggest a different angle or slant, or that a history piece be set in a different time frame. The reward of a good query letter is that the editor is aware of you for future purchases. (I normally follow a warm reply to a query, even if it's a rejection, with another query on a different subject fairly soon, while my name is fresh in the editor's mind. In the second query, I mention the topic of the first, in case it's the topic and not my name the editor recalls.)

A mimeographed rejection to your query doesn't necessarily imply that the query was poorly written. Some editors simply do not send personal notes. You will learn who they are, though hopefully your other queries will generate so much work that rejections in general will diminish and the impersonal denials will become sad memories of an early writing past.

Unfortunately, even poor queries sometimes draw personal replies, usually negative in result though harmless enough in tone. So a personal response isn't a reliable gauge as to the worth of a query. It says something, however. If you receive nothing but an unbroken string of faded, general rejections, take a hard look at what your queries are saying, how they are saying it, what they look like, and where they are being sent. Then ask yourself if the ideas you are trying to market aren't so limited in interest that there are too few readers to justify their being used.

Another thought about rejections is so obvious that

I would exclude it if I hadn't seen it so frequently violated: If an editor says no, don't try the same query with a different editor at the same publication. Good ideas are often discussed at regularly scheduled meetings of the general editorial staff. If your idea reached that level and was then rejected, the second editor would naturally follow suit. Even worse, there is usually just one editor who handles the type of manuscript you propose, so if you've already addressed that editor the first time and then tried another, the second submission will probably filter back to the first editor on the second attempt! In short, the only way to sell to that publication may be for the first editor to expire, flee, or retire, and it seems to be a rule in granite that any editor who rejects a query will never do any of the three, while editors who accept queries have the permanence of vapors.

STANDARD REJECTIONS

The form that standard rejections take is usually the blandest possible. "Sorry, this does not meet our present editorial needs. Thank you for considering us. Good luck in placing it elsewhere." Or something similar. Paltry stuff for your investment of time, brain power, postage, research, and hope. Still, it's better than writing the entire manuscript and then receiving the same unkind message.

REJECTIONS WITH TEETH

If you get a rejection with teeth, you probably earned it. I recall one from my own Dark Ages that says it all. I had tried to hawk a humorous short about motion sickness to an in-flight magazine. Not a surplus of brightness there! (Because it was humorous and a short, I sent the manuscript directly, without a query.) Imagine a passenger just settling back after a roller coaster takeoff, nausea bag in one hand, magazine in the other, launching into a laugh-filled ditty about the galling horrors of air sickness! I forget the editor's exact words. Some weren't in my writing vocabulary. Something about my ability to type in a straight-jacket, with the assurance that his competitor's magazine was the perfect place for such a revolting topic. Similar language can be expected when you try to sell pornography to church journals, abortion studies to *Jack and Jill,* and life-after-death pieces to retirement monthlies.

GO-AHEADS

The go-aheads are much more fun to read. "Let's see what you have . . ." is a common reply, scribbled in fourth-grade Palmer at the bottom of a query. Or "Send me the article on speculation." Never "This is the best query I've ever read. How can the manuscript be anything but better? Three thousand dollars enclosed. Rush copy—we are holding the next issue. How can we ever thank you for picking us?"

Actually, positive replies are often as bland as the rejections—with reason. You query *Slugger Magazine* about a new baseball bat that's being proposed. The editor, Bob Lester, reads your letter. He likes the idea and is enthused by the query. He thinks you can send accurate, well-written copy soon. But Bob doesn't know you. He doesn't want to promise too much in case the manuscript is unusable. He wants to encourage you to finish your research and write the text for his publication, but he doesn't want to risk cash on the outcome. He tells you to go ahead and he'll look at the result. No promise to pay. He has a thousand reasons why. Factors beyond his control. The magazine may fold. He may be flooded by better copy from his regular suppliers. The topic may appear in a competitive journal. His stockpile is filled. And so on.

The result is a bland go-ahead, with the true conditions unstated and hopefully not too obvious. You do the research and writing at your own expense, and if it meets his needs when he reads it, or later, he will make a commitment.

LEGALITIES

There's another problem too. If an editor says, "Yes, send me your article about ratfish (or whatever), I'll pay $500 for it," that editor has sealed a contract. The three elements of contract—offer, acceptance, and consideration—have been met. And if you send in the worst job imaginable, but about ratfish and on time, the editor owes you $500.

Mind you, getting the $500 might be a task, but legally you are in the right. The editor made no stipulation about quality or acceptance contingent on approval of the text.

This fact hasn't gone unnoticed by editors: Their first words to their replacements are, *"Don't say yes!"* Especially when they can say, "Let me see it," and get you to do the work at no risk and then make a decision when the product is in hand. Unfair? Fairness is an issue. But beginners trying to break into print and establish themselves as reliable wordsmiths who can produce for publication must accept the reality. Fairness here is for academics and lawyers, sadly. Bland go-aheads to queries, on speculation, are the reality for newcomers.

PAYING ON PUBLICATION

Those editors who pay on publication take it many steps further: They will pay, maybe, at some undefined time in the future if the publication still exists and the present editor is still around and something better hasn't come along to bounce the piece out of the pile, or until the facts are dated and the topic out of favor. For these reasons I never query a publication-payer, except with rewrites or reprints, when the main piece has already been sold and the time involvement on my part is slight. Then, if the article's used, it's all profit.

ABNORMAL REPLIES

If you write a good query, gird yourself for two kinds of replies: bland personal rejections, with an invitation to query again soon, or a fairly low key go-ahead, on spec. Anything else and I pay particular attention.

A printed rejection sets me to seeing what went wrong in my query and attempting to correct it the next time around.

A hearty acceptance that leaps beyond the bounds of blandness puts me to work quickly, to get the best possible manuscript in that editor's hands before he or she sobers up or the publisher catches on.

Any form of acceptance or go-ahead will result in more correspondence, of course. You must write a manuscript that lives up to the query's promises, altered to meet any suggestions by the editor in the go-ahead reply. The manuscript and supporting data (maps, photos, charts) should be sent by the time indicated.

MANUSCRIPT SUBMISSION REPLIES

The editor's second letter, announcing the fate of your submission, can take far longer than the response to the query. I figure a month at the second step, often longer. Sometimes the editor will acknowledge receipt of the manuscript. More often it is assumed that you know the procedure: The "package" you sent must be read by your editor, and often your editor's editor; the illustrations must be reviewed by the art or graphics editor, and so on. At the very least, the manuscript and attachments will be discussed again by the group at its regular meeting. The process takes time. Anxious time for you. Time to send other queries to other publications about other ideas.

Even then, after all your waiting, the reply may be negative. At that point, though, you have a right to expect a personal note rather than a printed rejection without comments. (If I received the latter, I'd write and ask why the material wasn't used. I'd also cross the publication off my list for future queries—for a year, at least.)

At times the manuscript will be rejected but the editor will suggest ways that it might be altered to be made usable. I act on those suggestions and do the rewrite as indicated, to save the time already invested in research and writing the original manuscript.

If the manuscript is rejected with a personal note, the reasons may sound limp: "No longer as vital a topic as before," "Reduction of copy space," or something similar. The editor may be letting you down softly. The manuscript may not be nearly as good as your query led the editor to expect. It lacks the vigor of the query, it has too little factual substance, you took a different slant or changed the conclusions . . . The editor doesn't want to discourage you totally, but the copy can't be used as is. Worse yet, the editor doesn't think you can bring it up to an acceptable level. The rewriting, the time, the letters, all take too much investment for too little certainty of yield. You blew it.

What do you do next? Query another publication, this time matching your promise to what you have to offer. Or send the actual manuscript to another publication, with a cover letter, as is or rewritten for the new readership. Don't say that it was already rejected elsewhere. Put the first editor on hold for a while, to let the sour taste leave both of your mouths, before querying that editor again. Don't mention the first manuscript in the subsequent query. Start fresh. Just don't forget that hard-learned lesson: The manuscript you send the editor must always be as good as the one you promised in a good query!

CHAPTER 15

Should You Send Simultaneous Queries to Different Editors?

There is only one limitation to the number of different queries about topics you should send out simultaneously or concurrently, and that is the number of pieces you can write should each editor say yes.

Naturally you shouldn't send a query unless you want to write about the item queried, so each letter must be your best effort to interest, and then sell, an editor.

Still, nobody succeeds with each letter, and it is absurd to assume that you are the exception. There are too many unknowns: what the editor has given go-aheads to from others' queries or what is already in type for the next or coming issues, what that editor abhors and will never use, what the competition favors and the editor avoids, and so on. So there will be rejections to the best-written queries.

DIFFERENT QUERIES

I try to keep at least 10 queries alive at a time, knowing that about a third will bring first-response go-aheads. About a third of the queries sent will be rejected outright, usually with a note saying why. The other third will fall into the delayed category, requiring follow-up correspondence. Sometimes a change in focus is requested, and the revision results in a later sale. Occasionally there is no reply. When I see that my writing load is backing up, I limit queries to those higher-priced markets I have sold to before.

SAME QUERIES TO DIFFERENT EDITORS

The usual question, though, doesn't refer to the situation we've just discussed, which is easy enough to comprehend. It refers to the number of queries on the same subject a writer can send simultaneously to different editors—a question that is harder to answer.

Again, a query is, in legal terms, an offer to sell a specific item to a publisher. You can sell an item as often as you wish. The problem comes when a potential purchaser wants to buy it with some degree of exclusivity. If that purchaser wants to buy all rights, you can sell it only once. If the buyer wants first rights, you can sell it elsewhere only after it has appeared in print on that editor's pages. In either case, you cannot initially sell the same rights simultaneously to different publications.

That's fine, you reply, but I know that if I query five times I'll be lucky to get one nibble, much less two bites, or sales, so what's wrong with shortening my odds and speeding up the process?

That's why the question is a hard one to answer.

What you are asking about is done, mostly by low-selling beginners.

It is risky—and skirts close to being unethical. Say that you do find the golden egg and have three hungry editors panting after the same gilded shell. To query and sell either to more than one editor or to the highest bidder, you may have to wriggle out of two potential sales, pretending their replies never arrived, in the hope that the third will in fact buy your manuscript at a stated or presumed rate; or you can write two or three pieces so similar that none of the editors, if they find out, will hire you again; you can think up a half-dozen other such profitless, amateurish derivations.

Worse yet, hard as it is to imagine, editors have friends. Other editors may be old college colleagues or next-door neighbors, or members of their staffs may talk to one another. When each becomes aware that you have queried the other about the same topic, hard feelings—or at least some tough questions—may well result.

MULTIPLE QUERIES:
FINE IN SPECIFIC MARKETS

In some areas there is no difficulty with simultaneous queries. Newspapers, with the exception of ones with national distribution, limit their rights to the geographic areas in which they are circulated. Thus you could query newspapers in Chicago, Atlanta, and Boston at the same time, and sell to all of them. But don't query two Chicago papers or papers in nearby areas, like South Bend and Milwaukee.

Another area with limited circulation is in-flight publications, which serve a distinct segment of the country or world and usually do not object to your selling the same piece to other in-flights in non-overlapping areas. Regional and religious magazines also have limited distribution and can be queried in the same way.

THE DIFFICULTY IS WITH EXCLUSIVITY

It is foolish to run the risk of sending the same query letter to two or three national publications that purchase some degree of exclusivity. There are other, better ways to get additional income from the same idea.

Let me share an actual example, which is amplified in the sample query section in Appendix A.

In the late 1970s, while writing for major magazines about running, I became particularly interested in women in the post-50 category as their times came tumbling down. Three of the world's fastest women runners in that age-group then lived in California. A marathon run in less than three hours is a true accomplishment for any person, but the thought that a female quinquagenarian might cover 26.2 miles in that time seemed an impossibility—until the times of these top contenders began slipping closer and closer to it.

How could I approach a number of magazines simultaneously with an article about this feat? One way would be to send the same query to all of the magazines. A better, more professional way would be to look deeper into the topic and see how the same material might be worked from three or more different angles, and then query editors from those different points of view.

Possible slants might be (1) a short biography of

each of the three athletes, (2) a longer piece featuring all three and discussing the possibility of their running a marathon in less than three hours, or (3) an article discussing running in the post-50 set, using these women and perhaps their male counterparts as examples of graying excellence in racing flats.

Who would be interested in a biography of such a runner? For starters, a running magazine, so that's where I concentrated. The May 1979 issue of *The Runner* contains the result, a 1,000-word short, with photo, about Margaret Miller. (The piece was later published in a book by the same group. They queried me asking for permission to reuse it and pay me again!)

All three women were from California, so I sought a magazine with a California readership. The March 1979 issue of *Air California Magazine* ran an article about Miller, Carol Cartwright, and Ruth Anderson, with photos by my colleagues Skip Matheson and Steve Koletty.

I queried the retirement magazine about the "graying marathoners" but was too late: They were up to their singlets in stories about older joggers.

These are three obvious approaches to this topic. At least 10 more could have been built around this trio.

The point should be obvious. Almost any theme can be expanded into a series of related yet different articles for different markets, each worthy of its own querying campaign, each query sent for the purpose of achieving its own sale.

CHAPTER 16

Should You Query by Phone or in Person?

A few publications listed in the *Writer's Market* prefer telephone queries, but many more list a number with their addresses. Yet there's only one situation when I'd initiate my contact by phone with a publication that didn't specifically request it: if I had an item so hot it had to be used almost immediately.

Having said that, I once did use the telephone and wound up with nearly $1,500 in speculation go-aheads which, with one exception, turned into paid articles. I joined a gold-hunting expedition to the Oriente section of Ecuador on the headwaters of the Amazon (actually the tributaries of the Napo River), and on the long shot that we didn't find gold and I survived, I wanted to back up my investment with articles. The group was leaving in 10 days!

So I called a men's fraternal magazine and got story leads in Colombia and Ecuador. A travel magazine wanted an item about Bogotá, and a consortium of three religious magazines went together on a piece about missionary work in Ecuador in which each church was taking part.

A camping journal wondered about backpacking in the foothills of the Andes. I simply told each that I was headed that way, spoke Spanish like a native (in an area where most of the "natives" knew only Indian tongues!), and could handle my own photography. They provided the subjects, letters of introduction, and bountiful good will. The church group even advanced $100—a true and unrequested act of faith. Friends called it a miracle.

There was a hook, though. Each publication was located in the greater Chicago area where I then lived, and I had time to visit most of the editors in person, after the phone contact, to sound them out about the specifics they wanted in the overseas report. In all, this was quite the reverse of most query approaches.

SUPERFICIAL CONTACT

I counsel against telephone queries, except in rare and special situations like the one just cited, because the contact is too superficial and may be as easily forgotten as the go-ahead may have been given. I like to have a well-written letter on the editor's desk to be read at leisure and thought about before the editor replies. Even though the first letter may miss the target, good query letters are in themselves impressive. A quick phone call lacks that lasting impact.

WHY THE RUSH?

Few topics are so urgent that they require a quick reply. In fact, editors, being like me, usually resent being asked to respond immediately to a question that should be given considerable thought.

Degree of Seriousness

I take a go-ahead reply seriously and find that if my query letter has been thorough and professional, editors respond in the same frame of mind. I know from talking with them that they usually jot the topic and your name on the calendar in the month when your finished manuscript might be used. Phone queries don't get penciled in until you are known, usually through past items in their publications. And those past items usually began with written queries.

Advantages of Distance

A minor matter should perhaps be mentioned. There is a certain formality and safe distance to a query letter that has its virtues. Some people simply don't communicate well by phone. They may stammer or beat around the bush, they may be intimidated by the editor's name or position, they may have a voice that grates or dances over the octaves. Or they may be the type who think before writing but not before speaking, or think so slowly or fully they sound simple-minded to those who don't know them.

Your purpose is to draw the editor's attention to an idea you want to write about for his or her publication. A phone conversation may well distract from that purpose, and a well-written letter wouldn't. Why take a chance unless you must? When you know the editor, or the editor initiates the call, these factors become far less important.

QUERYING IN PERSON

Fortunately, it's impossible to query in person in most cases. The editor works in New York City or Chicago and you live in Seattle or Ginger Flats.

Even if you live down the street from the top dog, I'd resist the temptation to cut short the business approach until you have established a good working relationship. Even then I'd take special care to keep my writing contacts clearly that.

The reason is simple enough: You have a product to sell—your writing. That has little to do with your personality, good looks, or boundless charm. The editor doesn't need to like you to print your words. The chemistry takes place on the page, and the personalities between the idea and print are of little importance.

So why put your person in the way of your prose? The idea you want to sell must first catch the editor's interest, and your treatment of that topic is what matters. The editor is busy; you are eager to sell. If you pop into the office with an idea half-formed, or even fully formed, and the editor isn't ready to consider it, you cannot relive the moment that didn't work. A query letter, on the other hand, sits around until the person you must impress is in a receptive mood. Or so you hope.

More Advantages of Distance

There's another factor. If your prose is magic but your appearance is poison to the editor, there's little chance that your writing will be given a fair reading. You may be too tall or too short, too warty or too smooth, too young or too old, a buffoon or not funny enough. Worse yet, you may look exactly like the editor's twin brother, the one who got the looks and stole his way to fame. Once seen, you are pegged for life—and your words remain unbought.

It's better not to be seen at all, except in sparkling, witty, clear phrases certain to pull thousands of excited new readers to the publication. Then, if a meeting transpires, you have the saving grace of being part of the editor's success. Funny how much better you will look then!

WRITTEN PROOF

A final thought: What if the editor says, "Great, bar no expense," during the personal interview, and you invest precious time and funds to produce a masterpiece. You rush back to the office to deliver the gem and that eager visionary says, "No, sorry, can't remember the discussion. . . ." Or the editor has left the publication, and the replacement, busily wiping the slate, can't find anything on the desk about such a commitment. Such tales dot the freelancing landscape. Keep the queries and commitments in writing, from inception to completion.

You also need a go-ahead in writing to be able to deduct the incurred costs from your income for tax purposes, whether the piece is ultimately bought or rejected. But more on that later.

The best argument against getting an in-person, oral go-ahead is that after granting verbal approval, many editors then ask you for a written query!

CHAPTER 17

Should You Query Abroad?

For the experienced writer, selling abroad can be highly profitable, but for newcomers the cost, time delays, and lack of familiarity with the publications themselves usually make the venture unprofitable.

Canada is often the exception because copies of Canadian magazines and even the larger newspapers are available in major U.S. libraries or well-stocked news shops. It's easy to study the markets before querying.

When sample copies are unavailable, you must rely on the listings in the *Writer's Market* when attempting to match your ideas with the proper markets. If your query interests the editor, you can always ask for a back issue or two for guidance in manuscript preparation.

THE OTHER SIDE OF OVERSEAS SALES

I'm speaking from my own experience and that of perhaps 90% of my writing colleagues, who at best dabble at overseas sales. But there is ample evidence that the foreign market can be lucrative if a writer is able, gutsy, and willing to make some initial investment for a potentially large return.

Unfortunately, there is very little in print about how it is done, and I know too little to be of help. Keep your eye out for seminars at nearby colleges or for future books in the bookstore.

ENGLISH-LANGUAGE PUBLICATIONS

For those focusing primarily on the United States market, it's best to limit queries to English-language publications, unless you are completely fluent in a foreign tongue, including the slang and peculiar regionalisms sometimes needed to write salable copy.

Stamps

Other countries won't accept U.S. stamps to return your SASE any more than you would accept horse feathers as payment for your prose.

Sometimes you can buy stamps of other countries, plus receive a list of current mailing rates, at their embassies or consulates. Otherwise, International Reply Coupons are available to guarantee a letter's return, boat mail. For air mail, you need several of them—and they are relatively expensive. (Ask at the post office for the current rates and how the coupons are used.)

I usually ask friends traveling to Canada to pick up a stock of stamps for me, but I refuse to use the coupons. Instead, in those rare times when I query England, Australia, or New Zealand, I explain the folly of the coupons in my letter and rely on their good will, and purse, not to reply if they aren't interested in the idea but to let me know if they wish to see the manuscript, deducting the mailing costs from the final payment. If I hear nothing in 60 days, I query elsewhere.

Querying abroad now and then just doesn't work that well, so let me suggest two other approaches, with emphasis on the second.

Send Manuscripts

I sell "seconds" overseas, pieces that have sold in the United States yet have enough appeal to interest readers anywhere. Most of those, for me, are travel or general interest articles.

If a resale takes place, fine. If it doesn't, it is a small gamble since there is little or no rewriting involved. The only costs come from making a photocopy of the original, putting it in an envelope, and sending it boat rate with a cover letter explaining where the item was previously used. I also mention that there are no rights difficulties, and why there is no return postage. It might cost $1.50 in shipping and 15 minutes of photocopying and addressing, on the long shot that it will be used abroad and pay from $25 to $350. When photos are involved, I include a list of available prints or slides, with a copy of the caption sheets, and ask the editor to indicate which shots he or she would like to consider. The editor replies by mail (or sometimes calls), I send the photos, and eventually the payment arrives and the photos come back. Yet there's an easier way.

MARKET THROUGH SYNDICATES

There are sales houses that act as brokers between American writers and hundreds of markets abroad, some in English, many in foreign languages. They find the clients, make the sales pitch, handle the translations, reproduce the slides, and pay you when you least expect it. That nets you about half the income you would have made had you done all the work of generating the sale yourself. It's a bargain at 50%.

See the *Writer's Market* under "syndicates," and, if it's available at your library, the *Editor and Publisher Syndicate Directory.* Read the write-ups closely to make sure they sell to the types of publications you write for. Then either query them or send a full manuscript, with information about illustrations, where the item has already been in print (if it has), and any rights that others have purchased. Almost all of the syndicates listed are U.S.-based or have local offices, so stamps are no problem, and you can use a SASE. (An example of a letter to a syndicate appears in Appendix B.)

There's little that pleases new writers more than receiving a tearsheet or a copy of a magazine with their work in a language they've never seen written before—with a tidy check attached! Or receiving a quarterly payment sheet with foreign publications listed.

My experience with syndicates has been mixed. Some don't reply to queries or acknowledge the receipt of manuscripts, even when you contact them later. But most are attentive and quite frank. They reject more items than they accept, usually because the topics won't sell abroad or the photos are unusable. Twice I tried to market items directly that the syndicates had rejected. They were right. The foreign markets, at least those I contacted, weren't interested.

Selling abroad? Concentrate on the United States and Canada, and when those sources are exhausted (or you are), check with the syndicates. *Boa sorte.*

PART THREE

Query Letters— Books

CHAPTER 18

Book Queries

N onfiction books comprise 92% of the books bought by publishers and are queried before being written in all but a few cases. The exceptions—usually short books (50 pages or less) or juvenile books—are described later.

It makes no sense to write 100 or 500 pages of the last word on anything only to find out that nobody wants to publish it. If it's smart to test the article market first with a query letter so you can wrap the writing around the user's needs, it's 100 times smarter for a book!

But there are a few hitches.

One, the query will probably be two pages long rather than one. Too much to say, usually, for one page. You can keep it to two, a readable length, by appending supplements.

What kind of items would you attach to, or at least submit with, your longer query? An annotated table of contents or an outline, a one-page synopsis (if necessary), and a sheet of references and resources. Plus a SASE.

THE BOOK QUERY

A book query differs little from an article query in purpose or form except that it's longer and tries to sell a heftier product. You have an idea to sell, your book theme, and a person to sell as its writer, you—sometimes with a co-author or a band of fellow conspirators. Your letter must interest the publisher in financing the venture (see Query Letter 3 on pages 115–117).

The costs of including your article in a magazine are modest and are usually covered by the advertising income. But books are less blessed. It costs the publisher anywhere from $3,000 to $20,000 for a modest run of any book, plus that much again for promotion, a chunk more for overhead, 10% or so off the list (retail) price for your royalty, plus the cost of books as comps to make your book known to reviewers and distributors, and something (if anything's left) for profit. Mind you, that's their problem—and publishing is a profitable business, almost despite itself.

But it's your problem too when you try to convince an editor that he or she should invest that many thousand dollars, on the hope of a profit, in your idea and your prose. Book editors have a lot more questions, and they need a lot more up-front convincing.

So your query and its attachments must be designed to answer most of those questions, put you and your idea in the best professional light, and save you the greatest amount of precontract writing time.

Your query must first sell the idea—why others would buy a book to read about it, what is already in print about the topic and why your book would be bought rather than (or in addition to) the others available, who specifically would be most interested, how they can be made aware of your book (if that's not obvious), and why you should write it.

Tell the editor your credentials, expertise, access to others who know the topic well, and/or experience. You needn't have sung in the Met to write a book telling others how to succeed professionally in an operatic career, but you sure in blazes better have some interviews, either promised or completed, with those who have, and a long list of practical tips before you even think about that text. And you'd better let the editor know about that pool of information.

If you're writing the book with somebody else, tell the editor who is doing what, who is handling the contracting and who is the go-between, and just who is that other person anyway. If a committee is writing the book, God forbid, do the same for each member.

All that, plus the letter must make the topic come alive. It must have the same verve and zest your book will need to keep its readers awake and eager for more. It's a sure bet that if you can't keep a query letter moving and lively for two pages, 200 pages will be lethal. You will be judged by the query. Would you send a letter with half its words misspelled if you were seeking a teaching position in an English department? Would you send a letter that is confused and rambling and dull to ask for $10,000 to finance a book?

ATTACHMENTS: THE CONTENTS

The query letter sells the idea and you, as well as giving a general explanation of what the book is about. Yet to pass fair judgment, the editor (and a cadre of advisors, at some publishing firms, who must also review the proposal) must know how you will organize the topic.

Your organization is best explained by an outline or an annotated table of contents. An outline is easy to envision since every junior high school student is forced at some time to prepare one. It tells, in order, the topic, its main subdivisions, and their sub-sub-divisions. Usually with Roman numerals, capital letters, numbers—you remember.

Alas, many books don't tightly follow such a rational breakdown. And an outline tends to read and look like a skyscraper's supports in its first stages: thin, rigid, and not much in between.

I prefer an annotated table of contents. It's a table of contents, as if the book were completed, with an annotation—a sentence or two—explaining each chapter and how it relates to the main theme, plus, if necessary, a specific fact or two that adds some excitement to its contents.

SYNOPSIS

Send a synopsis—a condensation or summary, in one page, single-spaced. If you can't do it in a page, says the conventional wisdom, you don't have a handle on it. And you can't do it any better in five. What's the book all about? And how are you going to share that with the reader?

Often a synopsis can be given in the query letter, so there is no need to say the same thing again. If a synopsis is needed, just be sure that you say enough about the topic in the query to snag the editor's interest; then add that the topic will be explained more fully in the attached synopsis.

REFERENCE/RESOURCE SHEET

This sheet tells the editor, and others interested, where you are getting the book material! Few are so gifted or positioned that their prose is totally unique—or funneled from some higher source solely through them, claims notwithstanding.

Editors feel comfortable when books contain facts, quotes, and anecdotes that have some known origin. They like history that somebody else has heard about, and people quoted who really existed. That assures the editor that you are using, at least in part, recorded and known information. And it tells where your information comes from and how you got it.

The reference segment tells what written material was found where. Simply list the most important information in annotated bibliographical fashion— the annotation being a sentence or two telling how that information relates to the theme of the book.

The resource segment is composed of oral information. This generally refers to live interviews, but it can also mean tapes, speeches, or radio or TV shows. These are listed in annotated biographical fashion. The biographies identify the people and what qualifies them to speak about the topic. The annotation tells how what they say relates to the theme.

This page—it can be longer, if needed—is far more important than it might appear to be. Assuming a solid query, good organization, and a sensible synopsis, you will still be judged strongly by your sources. Does this page show familiarity with the newest research? Are the key names in the field here? Are the streams of wisdom from which you are drawing truly so, or are they weak, seasonal runoffs? Which is worthier of a $10,000 investment?

THE FOLLOW-UP . . .

Send a dynamic package—query, outline or contents, synopsis, references and resources—to the "best" market, following the 15-step querying approach used for articles, but expanded and slightly modified. When an eager editor begs for more, indicating that three solid chapters are all that separate you from a contract and certain glory (not to mention lucre), get to it. Write those chapters with the same devoted precision that produced the winning query. Can fame and fortune be far behind?

AND THOSE FEW EXCEPTIONS

Sometimes it just isn't worth the effort to produce such a multipieced query, such a lovely selling package, particularly if it's faster to finish the book itself and just take your chances.

The editors agree, and for very short tomes (say 50 pages or less) or for juvenile books (for readers in the lower grades), where the words are few and the illustrations many, simply prepare the finished product, attach a cover letter saying what is necessary to effect a sale, and that's it.

Other kinds of books also follow this form: cartoon books, anthologies (which can also be queried), humorous books, and any other publications where the material has to be seen in final form to be understood, loved, and published.

Sometimes a book in this category is sent in partial form, as in Query Letter 9 in Appendix A. Some of the text and illustrations are offered, with the rest promised quickly. But usually it is best to let the editor see the shorter masterpieces intact.

Query Letter 3

123 Main Street
Santa Maria, CA 93456
(805) 123-4567
Month 1, Year

Mr. Rolf Zimmerman
Editor, Action Books
2745 Del Vista Boulevard
St. Louis, MO 70000

Dear Mr. Zimmerman:

We need a new sports challenge that any person would be proud to achieve and most could. Certainly all would benefit from trying.

More important, we can launch this event, tell every person how to train for it, and explain to any group or organization how to be its sponsor—all in a 100-page tome that would put Action Books in the annals of sports history. (It should make you plenty of money too!)

The event and the book would be called *Run Your Age!* Nothing more complicated: The people run their age. But with a slight modification: It could be run in kilometers or miles, with the young (say 15 or under) limited to running in kilometers only (a kilometer is about ⅝ of a mile).

Running is as old as humankind. In the past 15 years, as you know, it has become fashionable for both sexes of all ages to run, for competition, for fun, or for something in between. But the craze is slowing down, the 10Ks are leveling off, and a bit of the sparkle is gone.

For the average person, like myself, a 46 year old without the time (or serious interest) to train for true competition, it quickly became clear that I'd never win a race, could only get a bit better than I was at my best time, would be fighting to maintain those speeds as I aged, and that I could get a kick out of running just so many races, short or long. Multiply me by the millions, subtract the limited number of fairly new runners each year who still have the awe and dream I/we had when we were a few months or years into the sport, and you will have enough to keep the races running—and millions more, ex- or occasional racers who still run, but for other reasons.

You see, running is for the swift, or so it has always been. But why? There are two elements at stake: speed and endurance. The longer races—the marathons and the ultramarathons—put both to their fullest test.

Why not a race that rewards endurance and determination and inner pride but ignores speed, making the only stipulation that the distance traveled must be run, not walked? When tired, one stops, and then runs again when ready.

And why not a goal that grows ever more demanding? Nature has made living harder the longer one does it. Why not the same for running? Why not make the goal increase in proportion to one's aging? Running 20 miles when one is 20, and 50 when one is 50? If that seems backwards it's because we are used to equating strength with youth, so a 20 year old should be able to run 20 miles far easier than a 50 year old can run 50. Indeed. That's the idea.

People need milestones to measure their worth. *Run Your Age!* provides a simple milestone, something to work toward, accomplish, and cherish. In a way that a win in a 10K can't. Running one's age needn't be qualified. Fifty miles is 50 miles, period. But winning a 10K begs the rest of the story: against whom and how many, when, what terrain, and so on.

I shan't belabor the point much longer. The concept is so simple it either makes sense or it doesn't. Yet I see a large company embracing this idea, making it their own, becoming sponsors of age runs nationwide, and acting as the clearinghouse for a list of all who achieve the goal— and the distributor of rewards (sweatshirts, plaques, certificates, etc.) to the achievers.

Our task, though, is to make the idea known, through a book. A book I want to write, I'd like you to publish, and I think will make an imprint on America, and then the world. The simple ideas are often the best, for in them are the germs of universal truth that all recognize and are inspired by.

My own experience. In print 900-plus times, mostly in magazines and newspapers, about general interest, travel, humor, and sports—running, in fact. In addition, I've written five books, edited seven more, own a publishing house, was a dean at the university level twice, directed a city recreation program for three years, organized another, headed the CARE program in parts of Colombia and Ecuador, played professional baseball, and much more. I'll send details if you're interested.

And I've run my age. First I ran a mile, then three, then six marathons. And three years back, when two friends told me they had run 40 miles when they were 40, I set out to run 44 one Tuesday morning and did it. I plan to run 47 next year. And I'm proud as a peacock of it—far more so than the 60 races in which I've competed and, on occasion (when the ranks were full of widows and children), I did well.

The annotated table of contents accompanying this query letter explains, in rough form, what such a book might contain. Since the idea has yet to be in print, and since I'm wide open to suggestions on the breadth of the text— should it be more specific on preparing to run one's age, should it be a workbook for sponsors on how to run the event, should it be both, should it contain model registration forms, etc.—it is simply a working outline. Yet in lieu of suggestions or other directions, it is how, at present, I propose to write the book.

The reference/resource sheet is skimpy because the topic is new. Yet there are some guidelines you might use to help you see that my proposal is not too far off base. And that I might use in the preparation of my text.

So that's it. Is the idea as exciting to you as it is to me? Do you see it as a book your firm wants to print, Mr. Zimmerman? Or do you see a way that the idea could be presented in an even better book?

Please let me know. Thousands are growing too old to reach their age by foot while we dally!

Many thanks,
Gordon Burgett

Annotated Table of Contents for *Run Your Age!*

I. Run Your Own Age

Explains the concept, why it is being proposed, that it is an open challenge to all, where and when it can be done, the few restrictions (the distance must be run, in miles or kilometers, and no times are recorded), and any anecdotal or historical information encountered to reinforce or explain the concept.

II. How One Prepares

A general review of the basics of running, drawn from the many texts and references in this field. Who shouldn't attempt the challenge. Of those who should, or could, how they would work up to the level where such a run would be sensible. And then a solid review of the running books now available, in annotated bibliographical fashion, to emphasize the points each makes from which the potential age runners would benefit.

III. The Day of the Event

How one faces the task, mentally and physically. Prerun preparation. Needed support. Water stops, aid backups or contacts. A mental framework that will make the task more enjoyable—or endurable. And what one does when one finishes, on or short of the mark. Postrun rest and recuperation. And how you brag gracefully to your friends!

IV. Sponsoring an Age Run

Promotion, site selection, route measurement, marking, aid stations, medical and traffic help, necessary approvals, support wagons, water and nutrient stops, washrooms, dressing room and equipment (extra clothes, shoes, Vaseline, etc.) storage, running verification, awards, postrun publicity. Everything but clocks.

Reference/Resource Sheet for *Run Your Age!*

References

There are no direct references from which one can draw information or guidance about this concept since the idea has yet to appear in print. However, from the following books one can find evidence, if it is needed, that running one's age is possible and that the organization of such an event is feasible:

Bloom, Marc, *What It Takes to Go the Distance,* Holt, Rinehart and Winston, 1981.

Edwards, Sally, *Triathlon,* Contemporary Books, 1983.

Glasser, William, *Positive Addiction,* Harper and Row, 1976.

Montgomery, David, *The Triathlon Handbook,* Leisure Press, 1983.

Perry, Paul, *Complete Book of Triathloning,* New American Library, 1983.

Sheehan, George, *Running and Being: The Total Experience,* Simon and Schuster, 1978.

Sheehan, George, *This Running Life,* Simon and Schuster, 1980.

There are additional marathoning books by Nathan Aaseng, Bob Anderson, Gayle Barron, Richard Benyo, Skip Brown, Gail Campbell, Julianne Fogel, Hal Higdon, John Humphreys, Bill Rodgers, Jim Shapiro, Manfred Steffny, and Cliff Temple.

Resources

Whereas references refer to written material, resources (in this case) refer to people I would interview to gain information about the following topics:

1. the feasibility and advisability of having people run their age

2. the psychological value of having such a goal known to all
3. the logistics of conducting such an event
4. the value and advisability of running the event "on one's own," with one's own backup support, versus doing so at an organized event

In the first case I would interview, if needed, those who have run marathons or ultramarathons, particularly runners 40 and over.

For the second item I would pose the question to sociologists, cultural anthropologists, psychologists, and others whose primary interest—and writing or speaking—focuses on values.

I would ask the third resource folk—those who have administered similar running events, such as marathons or ultramarathons—what changes from their regular procedures they would recommend, what guidebooks they used in their own administration, and what advice they would offer.

The fourth category is the most difficult since, to my knowledge, such an event has not been held. Thus one has no basis of comparison for such an answer. The question, however, might be posed to all those interviewed in categories (1) through (3) to see what insights, if any, they might shed on the choice of the best way to run one's age.

PART FOUR

Cover Letters

CHAPTER 19

What Is a Cover Letter?

A cover letter is a letter one page or longer that accompanies copy already written or photos being submitted. It usually includes information about what is being sent, why, how it might be used, sources consulted for its preparation, special knowledge or preparation one employs in its research and writing, the availability of additional items (like photographs), and other related facts.

It differs from the query letter, which is written to the editor before the copy is prepared.

WHEN DO YOU SEND A COVER LETTER?

Let's say you meet an inventor who is putting the finishing touches on a translating computer. He types a letter on the keyboard in English, enters a code for any of a dozen languages, and in a few seconds that message appears on the monitor in the chosen tongue.

Even better, the inventor is eager to let the world know of his invention!

So you write a query letter to *Ideas International*, a hot new magazine on the stands. The editor is wild for the article! You complete your research, conduct several interviews, take some photos, and zip the copy her way.

She knows the manuscript is coming, so you don't need a cover letter for that purpose. But you do have to include some comments about the use of the photos, you think you should divulge the origin of some of the more bizarre facts, and you want to be sure that the typesetter spells the inventor's first name "Roberrt" correctly—so you send a cover letter with the copy.

Thus it's possible that you could send both a query and a cover letter to the same editor.

But it's far more likely that a cover letter will accompany material for which there is no query. For fiction, a cover letter may be sent with a short story or a novel. For nonfiction, cover letters often accompany simultaneous, direct, or syndicated submissions, reprints, fillers, or photos.

TO WHOM SHOULD THE COVER LETTER BE SENT?

Send your cover letter to the editor or person who is the most appropriate recipient of the item that accompanies the cover letter. If a query letter preceded the manuscript and cover letter submission, send the letter to the same person indicated in or responding to the query.

When you are submitting the material and the cover letter for the first time, check the current issue of *Writer's Market* and send your items to the appropriate editor.

WHAT DOES A COVER LETTER LOOK LIKE?

A cover letter is a business letter not dissimilar in appearance from a query letter. For form, refer to Chapter 24. A cover letter's contents depend on why it is being sent and are better discussed under the various categories that follow. Yet all cover letters must be well-written, clear, grammatically proper, and with correct spelling—in every way the best possible demonstration of your writing ability.

Remember, the editor has relatively little evidence of your writing. You've previously sent a query letter. Or only the copy attached to the cover letter. From those limited examples, the editor must decide whether to purchase your prose.

You could flood that editor's mail with other examples, of course, but that wouldn't do. Just make sure that every item you put before his or her eyes displays your writing skills in the best professional light. Why? Because a well-written article accompanied by a poorly written cover letter—creative spelling, crazy asides, grammar from another planet—may well be rejected. It simply raises too many doubts in an editor's mind.

CAN YOU SEND SIMULTANEOUS COVER LETTERS?

Sure. If you are sending simultaneous submissions or reprints you can produce a master letter and send copies with each submission or reprint. We'll dwell on each of these categories next and will suggest times when simultaneous cover letters, while proper, might be more effective if replaced by a personal cover note.

SIMULTANEOUS SUBMISSION COVER LETTERS

Simultaneous submissions can usually be sent to editors of newspaper travel sections or of weekly newspaper supplements, as well as to editors of in-flight, religious, or regional magazines. The rule of thumb is that you cannot send the same submission to publications whose circulation, distribution, or readership overlaps.

NEWSPAPER TRAVEL COVER LETTERS

For newspaper travel sections, for example, you could send the same item to, say, the *Los Angeles Times*, the *Chicago Tribune*, and *Newsday*, on Long Island, since none comes close to overlapping another. But you could not send it to the *Wall Street Journal* or the *Christian Science Monitor*, for example, and any other newspaper, since the *Journal* and *Monitor* are national and overlap all the others.

Querying here seldom works because travel editors are too busy to play the correspondence game. If you have a travel item or an article you think their readers would enjoy, send it, with a SASE. Then forget it.

Newspaper travel sections pay on publication, which can be a week or a year after receipt of your copy, and the pay for copy without photos is modest, from $80 to $125. But you can make a dozen copies of an article (best length, 1,000 to 1,600 words) and send them to scattered newspapers at the same time. The chance of selling the piece three or four times offsets the pay range and the risk of submitting without a go-ahead response to a query.

Let's say that you have written an electric 1,400-word gem, a travel piece so good that you are sure editors will stop the press to put it in the earliest possible edition! And you decide to give the lucky millions in L.A., Chicago, and the greater New York City area the chance to see this prose in their local newspapers.

So you make three clean copies of each page of your manuscript, collate them, and find three manila envelopes into which you insert an unfolded article and a SASE for each editor.

Do you need a cover letter? Isn't it obvious why the contents are being sent? Won't the SASE get the response you desire?

If you have nothing more to say, a cover letter isn't mandatory. You can simply mail the material and wait for the money truck.

But why not take every advantage to sell your prose and other, related income stretchers? Why half-sell when a note could make a major difference, perhaps even double the editor's ante?

Suggested Format

Let's say that your magic prose concerns Santa Barbara, California, and you are sending it to *Newsday*'s travel editor. Furthermore, you have both black-and-white photos and color slides.

You might prepare a cover letter like Cover Letter 1.

Cover Letter 1

Gordon Burgett
123 Main Street
Santa Maria, CA 93456
(805) 123-4567
Month 1, Year

Dear Mr. Johnson:

"Where the Westerns Were Born and the Stars Now Hide" can only be Santa Barbara, California, site of the earliest Flying A shoot-'em-ups and the hidden haven, in its secluded canyons and Montecito niches, of many of today's top film, stage, and concert stars. The 1,400-word article, attached, tells your readers how to find the remnants of the Flying A, where the stars come out at night, and how they can blend the resort's natural bounty of surf, sun, and wilderness with the well-preserved relics of a rich historic past, fine cuisine, and a thriving night life.

I also have about 100 good-to-excellent b/w's to select from, if you're interested. Let me know and I'll send the 16 best, for your choice. (Also available are 36 slides so alluring you will want to abandon the New York tundra on the spot!)

Please don't return the ms, just your verdict in the SASE.

Thanks,
Gordon Burgett

I write this type of cover letter on precut paper that is only 5¼" long. (It can be 8½" wide or less.) I didn't include an inside address because the letter has to be kept short, so that when I staple it to the first page of the actual manuscript, it covers only the title, the byline, and the word count. (I staple newspaper submissions but use paper clips for magazine submissions. The first are simply treated with less care so I want to make certain that all the pages stay together.)

I begin the actual copy on the middle of the first page of the manuscript. That way the editor will read my cover note first and will be so enchanted by my summary of the article's contents and the promise of eye-boggling photos that he or she will continue reading the manuscript that begins where my note ends. The natural conclusion would be a quick note (probably on the back of my cover letter) asking for the b/w's as soon as possible, mailed that day in my SASE. (I would respond the moment the request was received lest the Long Islanders be deprived of this article even one hour longer than absolutely necessary.)

Note the contents of the cover letter. My address, phone number, and the date appear at the top. The phone number makes me instantly accessible if the editor has a question or wants to use the material immediately.

The first paragraph describes the article attached, in much the same tone as the copy itself. If the piece is humorous or light, so is the opening. If it's somber or heavily factual, that first paragraph follows suit.

The opening paragraph is what sells your copy. If you can't ignite a spark of interest and highlight the key factor(s) in your piece in those first words, the editor may simply set it aside. So the opener, like the lead in an article, must tickle that interest and make the editor want to read more.

The second paragraph tells what photos you have for sale and how you will make them available to the editor. Since black-and-whites are by far the most sought after by newspaper travel editors, mention them first. You don't want to tie up all of your photos with one editor, so offer to send a selection, say 16, or even the 5 best.

Should you have a photo so noteworthy it may rival the copy for inclusion on the travel page, you may wish to expand upon it in the second paragraph. A shot of a housewife watching in awe as her dime slot machine belches out $5,000 might highlight a piece on hitting the gambling meccas in New Jersey or Nevada.

The third paragraph is a personal preference. It strikes me as unpatriotic to make my uncle, Sam, unduly fat from postal proceeds from returning unusable manuscripts. Why pay to get a rejection back when it will be folded and bent so badly it can't be sent to another editor? Rather, a single first-class stamp on a small envelope gets the reply I need.

There's another way to get a reply that's even less expensive and just as effective. Include a self-addressed, stamped postcard with boxes to check and a space on the bottom for comments and editor identification. Here's an example:

Submission: _____

☐ Yep, am holding for possible future use.

☐ Let's see your b/w photos.

☐ Let's see your color slides.

☐ Not this time!

☐ Comments:

Name _____

Publication _____

Should Travel Cover Letters Be General?

The first time you are mailing to various newspaper travel sections and you don't know the editors' names, you can write a general cover letter, making certain not to distinguish it with geographic or specific comments. Note that the example in Cover Letter 1 mentions New York and includes the editor's name. In the general note you would address it to Dear Travel Editor—and omit such specifics. (You will know the editors' names from the responses to this first mailing!)

But it makes more sense to prepare the travel cover letters for each editor and attach them to the manuscripts that are mass produced. Editors are people too, and, like you, they respond better when called by a name and spoken to directly. And over time you will come to know them, indirectly, and will have particular comments to add.

It's easy enough to write a master cover letter, circle each item that must be personalized, and type the individual letters quickly or program them into your word processor, with inserts.

Final Thoughts About Newspaper Travel Cover Letters

These are kept short because the copy is attached. It's obvious why the material is being sent (you want fame and fortune by having it appear in the newspaper) and how it might be used. The sources consulted and special skills you brought to it are less important: The editor can read it to see if its content is acceptable.

The note here is sent to provide a short selling summary and to interest the editor in other support items for sale, like photos. Keep it interesting, quick, and to the point.

Do You Use This Short Form for Other Simultaneous Submissions?

No, because it is designed to meet the needs of newspaper submissions. Its brevity works particularly well in this case, and most other cover letters simply need more words to do more things. In fact, it won't always work even for the cases we've cited in this section. When they too require more space than it affords, a full-page letter is advised.

OTHER SIMULTANEOUS SUBMISSION COVER LETTERS

The form of cover letter described for submissions to newspaper travel editors won't usually work for the other major types of simultaneous submissions: newspaper weekly supplements and in-flight, regional, or religious magazines.

Newspaper Weekly Supplements

These are generally the magazinelike inserts distributed with newspapers, usually on Saturday or Sunday. Some, like *Parade Magazine* or *Family Weekly*, are national in distribution, though they appear in the local newspaper. Others are produced by a newspaper itself, like the *Dallas Life Magazine* (the Sunday magazine of the *Dallas Morning News*) and the *Boston Globe Magazine* (the Sunday magazine of, yes, the *Boston Globe*. You can find these, plus valuable information about special editions and sections, in the *Editor and Publisher Yearbook. Working Press of the Nation*, also in your library, will tell you the names of both the travel editors and the weekly supplement editors.

If you send the copy to a national supplement, you cannot submit it to another national or local supplement, unless the first submission is rejected. Remember, you must limit simultaneous submissions to newspapers that do not overlap in circulation or distribution.

Yet if you restrict submission to local supplements only, and if these are sufficiently far apart, the process is not unlike that used for newspaper travel articles.

A full-page letter is probably more appropriate in this case because the cover may well require more content. It should also be individually written, like one you would write for higher-paying magazine submissions.

The contents of the letter depend entirely on what needs to be said about the accompanying copy. How or why it might interest local readers usually has highest priority with the editor, for local weekly supplements are overwhelmingly interested in local or regional matters.

The way you can circumvent this difficulty, if you hope to distribute the same piece nationwide, is by focusing the article on a topic that appeals to residents everywhere. Editors are particularly receptive to humor or humorous pieces when the topic is broad.

The letter might explain the origin of the material cited, the author's expertise for discussing the topic, the availability of illustrations or photos, or other matters that would help sell the copy.

Again, the writing in the cover letter and the overall professionalism in its composition are extremely important. The editor will read the cover letter first. Will that editor even bother to look at the attachment if the cover letter looks as if it was composed by an illiterate or a reveler in search of sobriety?

While most newspaper supplement editors will assume that you are submitting your article to other, similar publications outside of their orb, you can either indicate *simultaneous submission* on the manuscript below the word count (in the upper right-hand corner of the first page) or you can explain this in the cover letter.

Simultaneous Submissions to In-Flight, Regional, and Religious Magazines

In general, what has been said about newspaper travel and weekly supplements concerning where and when simultaneous submissions can be sent applies to these three magazine categories. You can send the same manuscript to in-flight magazines that do not overlap—that is, whose airlines do not serve the same geographic area. So you could send the same item to regional lines each serving the Northeast, Alaska, Mexico, the South, and Hawaii, but you could not send it to a national or world carrier, say to United or American Airlines, and to any other airline serving the same markets at the same time.

The same holds true for regional magazines. A piece on the name "Portland" could be sold to regional magazines in Oregon, Indiana, and Maine, but not simultaneously to a national magazine with readership in any of the three states.

Religious magazines generally feel that their readership comes from their own flock, so if you could find a topic—God knows what!—that would appeal to, say, the Dunkards, Unitarians, Mormons, and the

Hardshell Doubters, you could send it to a publication of each of those sects or faiths. But if the HDs have five magazines, you must send it to each, one at a time, since their readership does indeed overlap.

Mind you, it is important to check the current *Writer's Market* to see if each of the publications in the three fields being discussed does in fact buy simultaneous submissions. Unless *Writer's Market* states to the contrary, assume that each does.

Again, the contents of the cover letter accompanying your copy will differ according to the needs that letter must meet or the information it must express. The letters should be written individually on full-size paper, and each editor will have at least one key question: Why would my readers be interested in this topic?

It is imperative that manuscripts that are simultaneously submitted to magazines clearly state the words *simultaneous submission*. If necessary, you can either further delineate the breakdown at that point—such as "Dunkard copy," "Northwestern U.S. copy," or "Hawaiian Airlines copy"—or you can explain that delineation in the cover letter itself.

As with all submissions or queries, a SASE should accompany the items sent.

CHAPTER 20

Reprints

Reprints are the reuse of copy already in print, in its original form or slightly modified. That is, you sold a manuscript to a publication on a first-rights basis. It appeared in print, and you submit it to one or many other publications, one at a time or simultaneously, to be reprinted. (It can be sent to many markets because there is no exclusivity in the use of reprints.)

When you submit copy as a reprint, you have three obligations. You must tell which publication bought the first rights, when it appeared in print in that publication, and that you are offering the editor to whom it is being sent either reprint or second rights. (The terms are interchangeable; there are no third or fourth rights.)

And that's it. The rest the editor should know. That there is no exclusivity, that you can offer it to the competition, that it may have been read by that publication's readership elsewhere, that you have already been paid once for this journalistic jewel, and that you hope to be paid many times more for the same display of literary dexterity.

WHAT SHOULD A REPRINT SUBMISSION COVER LETTER CONTAIN?

Enough to fulfill your obligation and get the piece bought. Since the original manuscript must be in print before reprints can be offered for purchase by other editors, why not take a copy of that published original, cut and paste it up so it can be presentably copied, and make as many clean copies as you wish to hawk?

Then send that copy of the article with your cover letter, letting the cover letter refer to the printed sample while it expands on the virtues of its contents and composition, tells the rights being offered, mentions the availability of photos or slides, and suggests that a copy can be sent for their typesetter's ease, as Cover Letter 2 shows.

Cover Letter 2

---

123 Main Street
Santa Maria, CA 93456
(805) 123-4567
Month 1, Year

Mrs. Bernice Elston
Articles Editor, *Spring News*
666 Albatross Avenue
Burlington Junction, MO 60000

Dear Mrs. Elston:

How many of your readers are certain that they can write better greeting cards than those on the racks? How many would like to earn $60 or $70 for writing just the lines?

The enclosed article tells them how to prepare and sell their own ideas to the major U.S. firms that buy from the public.

It discusses what is being bought, which companies are currently buying, how they should be approached, and when to submit material for seasonal and everyday cards. Even more crucial, it tells what the cards must contain, the three-word magic formula, and why some cards sell while others don't.

Editors from three top companies are quoted and anecdotes about freelance writers are included. The facts are current, and the box following the prose lists the top 20 markets—each with an address, the editor's name, and the kinds of cards each firm prefers.

Most important, since humor is what most greeting card editors want, humor is what this piece offers, consistently and gently. But the contents are serious: I've sold hundreds of comedy lines, to virtually every company listed (though most to Hallmark), so I know that you can laugh while you write, but it takes diligence and purpose to sell.

The article enclosed first appeared in the *Whittle Airline News* in May 1983, so I am offering you second rights. The photos and the greeting card illustrations were sold on a one-time rights basis and are available for you to use again. I also have 24 additional slides and an assortment of 40 cards from which you can select other illustrations, if you're interested.

It is difficult to edit or typeset from a printed article, so should you wish to publish this piece, I'll gladly send you a copy of the original, double-spaced manuscript. Just let me know.

A nebbish on the outside of the card shouts, "You're a saint! History will immortalize you for the contribution you're making to society . . .

. . . by laughing at these stupid cards!" finishes the inside.

The fun and funds somebody earned by writing and submitting that line, seeing it appear at the store, and even sending it to friends could be shared by many of your readers. Shall we tell them how?

Gordon Burgett

WHY USE THIS KIND OF LETTER?

Editors are busy, and a letter like this gets your task done quickly with the greatest amount of both sales appeal and follow-up acumen.

Starting off with a paragraph or several that summarize the contents and purpose of the article, written in the style or tone of the actual prose, gets right to it. You answer the questions the editor has: Why are you writing me, what does the attached item contain, why should I (and my readers) care, and is it worth my time to read?

So make the opening paragraphs good reading, concerning a subject the editor's readers care about, written with enthusiasm and an economy of words, and sufficiently alluring so the editor will want to read the whole article.

The short paragraph that follows tells the terms. The article first appeared in such-and-such a publication on X date (article copy enclosed), and you are offering second (or reprint) rights for its use. Those three elements are mandatory—but no more are needed. You don't have to reveal that you are also offering it to 732 other publications, that the first editor barely bought it—after 17 rewrites, or that the reprint, if bought, will pay more than the original sale!

If prints or slides are available—if you have them or can get them—an additional paragraph mentioning them can add substantially to your coffers and to the material's desirability. Since illustrative material is usually sold on a one-time rights basis, and its purchase with the original manuscript used up those rights, you can offer the same items for sale again, as well as other items the first editor wasn't wise or greedy enough to gobble up with your original sale.

Tell of the availability of your prints, slides, maps,

charts, whatever. If any are particularly good or vital, expand upon them: their quality, uniqueness, and/or crucial importance to understanding the text. And offer to send them for the editor's review for possible purchase with the copy.

The next paragraph seems harmless enough. You offer to send a copy of the original manuscript—double-spaced, wide left margin—for the typesetter's benefit since it would be far easier to use than the folded and tight-spaced article copy sent with the cover letter.

Compassion aside, that lets you keep an eye on those publications most likely to reuse your prose. Editors requesting a copy of the manuscript will as often as not put it into print. Which should mean that more welcome funds find their way into your pocket. Yet the publications most likely to use reprints are, sadly, those most likely not to pay, at least quickly. So by knowing where your words are most likely to appear, you know where to look. You can cast an occasional eye on the newsstand or at the library to see if your item saw light, and if necessary send a gentle reminder of non- or slow payment.

Most pay-on-publication magazines do just that, promptly. But if a month has passed since the item appeared in print, I'd drop the editor a note complimenting the good job done with your piece in the recent issue. Find something to commend. Then note that the check was probably mailed but has yet to arrive. Thank the editor for using your piece. A month later and no check, forget the compliments!

WHO BUYS REPRINTS?

Any publication can buy reprints, but the higher priced ones seldom do. And if a publication pays on acceptance, it's to your advantage to query and prepare an original manuscript when you receive a positive response to your query, as the professionals do. But those that pay on publication are ideal for re-print submissions. Professionals don't query them. It's not worth the time for such a vague and delayed possibility of use and payment. But items already sold that lend themselves to resale are indeed worth the time and effort to market this way. All the better, because almost all pay-on-publication markets seek and buy reprints.

HOW DO REPRINTS DIFFER FROM SIMULTANEOUS SUBMISSIONS?

In one sense, reprints can be simultaneous submis-sions. Once the item has appeared in print, you can market it simultaneously if you wish, since it has no exclusivity and your cover letter will indicate that it is a reprint (or for second rights).

But reprints differ from newspaper and magazine simultaneous submissions, as mentioned elsewhere in this section, because with reprints the copy has already appeared in print, locally or nationally. What you are offering the editor is the opportunity to use it again, without regard to possible market overlap. That is the editor's concern as long as you have clearly indicated that what you are selling is a reprint or for second rights. Nor should you mark *simultaneous submission* on the manuscript.

HOW MUCH DO THEY PAY FOR REPRINTS?

The pay for reprints varies according to the purchaser, but it's almost always less than that for the original manuscript, often 75% or even 50% of the rate of first-appearance material.

With photos or illustrations, though, you can often equal and sometimes surpass the amount paid for an original.

WILL REWRITING A REPRINT INCREASE ITS VALUE?

Usually, but it also increases your working time, so the question for you is whether the extra minutes or hours are compensated for by the increase in pay—especially since your markets will probably pay on publication. If they use the item at all, your pay will be longer in coming.

If the editor will use the item only if it is rewritten, you must decide if it's worth doing based primarily on those criteria. Sometimes it's possible to get a firm commitment from a pay-on-publication editor that either the piece will indeed be used or that you will, in that particular case, be paid upon its acceptance.

CAN YOU SEND THE SAME LETTER TO EVERY EDITOR?

The same basic copy, yes. I'd change the name in the greeting, of course. Editors are so human they like to be addressed by their own names!

When you know that a publication has specific needs that your copy addresses, you might change your cover letter to reflect that. If you know that an editor, for example, eagerly seeks good slides for his or her cover to match the key story, you might well mention some particularly good slides that could serve that purpose. If your piece would be of interest to oculists or octogenarians, and if your editors cater to those readers, draw attention to the tie-in between what you wrote and what their audience reads.

But otherwise a dynamite letter, well-directed to even the crustiest of editors, should blast loose the rustiest of purselocks. A solid sales letter promoting good, needed copy, even secondhand, should be altered only when the changes make it an even better sales tool.

IS THERE A DIFFERENCE BETWEEN REPRINTS AND SECOND RIGHTS?

Only a minor semantic difference. A reprint sometimes refers to an article or printed item being an absolute or near-exact copy of an original. But when one refers to rights the terms are identical: Reprint rights and second rights are the same.

CHAPTER 21

Fillers

Most fillers are short items produced in manuscript form with the word *filler* written under the word count in the upper right-hand corner of the first page. They are sent with a SASE to the Filler Editor. Few require a cover letter.

After all, the Filler Editor (if such a person actually exists) knows what you want: to be paid a king's ransom for a short gem or several paragraphs of wit or clarion insight.

So send a cover letter only in those rare cases where it is necessary to say something more than (1) I am enclosing a nearly priceless piece of writing, (2) please pay me top price for it nevertheless, (3) instantly, and (4) let me know your decision even sooner!

When might a cover letter be necessary with a filler? In one of the following instances:

1. The item includes information not well-known or subject to question by the editor. You can cite the source in a cover letter or even at the end of the material itself. If it's truly shocking, you might even make a copy of the source and include that as part of or attached to the cover letter.

2. You can provide photos or illustrative material related to the filler. That too could either be noted on the filler itself or explained, probably in greater detail, in the cover letter.

3. You want to offer additional information about the filler or related fillers. For example, tell the editor that you could expand the item to a full article or that you could provide other such items regularly or as a column if the editor is interested.

4. You have other necessary comments concerning the filler or fillers that would be more appropriate in an accompanying letter.

If a cover letter isn't necessary, just send in the copy. A superfluous letter costs postage, wastes the editor's time, reflects poorly on your wisdom, and detracts from the only true purpose of your submission—selling your short filler gem.

CHAPTER 22

Syndication

The lines between a query letter and a cover letter grow fuzzy in this category, as they do when you submit children's or very short fiction (described elsewhere). In a query, you send the letter before you write the material; in a cover letter, after. So in some ways you do both when contacting a syndicate.

A bit of background first will make this clearer. Instead of writing an article and submitting it directly to an editor or, better yet, querying and writing once you have a go-ahead, you contact a syndicate, a broker, a go-between, that receives your material and sells it to one or several publications.

HOW SYNDICATES SELL

Most syndicates work the domestic market, with an occasional sale abroad. Some work outside the United States exclusively. Some buy single features and/or serials. Many prefer ongoing columns.

So you must study your markets in the current *Writer's Market* or the *Editor and Publisher Syndicate Directory* and submit according to their needs and your interests.

SINGLE FEATURES

Single features, or even a series of several items about the same topic, are bought, but less often or widely than columns. How you submit to syndicates with these items depends on whether the material is new or is being offered for reprint.

If you wish to sell an article or series that is new, that you have never had published in that form or perhaps never even written, you can either follow the standard querying approach or you can do the actual writing and send the copy to the syndicate. The query or cover letter will be the same as any other such letter, with the exception that the wording will discuss syndication rather than single-market submission. Another obvious deviation: Why would many markets be interested in this topic?

ARTICLE REPRINTS

If you have already sold one or several articles, say in the United States and Canada, and you think that markets outside of North America would also be interested in that material, you can send the articles, singly or together, to syndicates that work such publications abroad.

In this case your cover letter will differ little from a standard reprint cover letter, except that you must indicate all of the publications that have used the article(s) and offer the syndication either overseas rights or those for a particular area or language.

Syndicates working the foreign markets are particularly interested in prints and slides, so be explicit here: precisely what you have—number and quality.

You might also ask, in a querying fashion, if there

are other topics they are seeking at the present time. Finally, cover letters to syndicates often contain more information, thus need more space. The one-page guideline for most such letters usually needs to be relaxed here to take care of all the business in one writing.

COLUMNS

Columns are where the query and cover letter become one.

Most syndication editors want to see a selection of columns, 6 or 10 in number ranging from 500 to 1,000 words long, to evaluate your writing skills and to have an offering to show prospective clients among the newspapers and occasional magazines that the syndicate serves. The clients want to make the same evaluation.

Furthermore, should you reach an agreement that requires you to provide a new column on a daily, weekly, or monthly basis, the syndicate wants at least some early indication that you can indeed write about the same general theme from 6 or 10 different approaches. And, finally, should you not live up to your part of the agreement or even fall behind schedule, the syndicate can draw from these 6 to 10 columns to temporarily fill the gap.

What you send with those first samples concerns us here.

Since the sample columns accompany your first letter, it is a cover letter. But it is also a query, because its purpose is to sell your idea (a new column) and yourself (as the writer of the columns). The sample columns show how you would approach the idea and what writing skills you bring to the task. And the crucial question is whether that syndicate will represent you in the sale of those literary jewels—and the thousands to come—so they can be read by the masses everywhere.

Thus the letter does what a query must do. It must sell your idea and you. And to do that it must be written as well as the items to be sold. It must

1. explain your column concept clearly
2. tell why readers would want to know about it
3. indicate which readers would be particularly interested
4. list other columns or information now available to them about the topic
5. tell how your column will provide that information better: more current, easier to understand and apply, wittier, drawn from wider sources
6. explain your credentials and how they relate to this column
7. list your publications and other evidences of idea dissemination, emphasizing those most closely related to the column idea
8. indicate any following you or your publications have among professional peers, laymen, or others likely to be drawn to the column for that reason
9. show a keen interest in writing the column and how it can be worked into your already busy professional schedule so that deadlines will be faithfully met
10. explain anything else needed to sell your idea and you as the person to bring it to the public in print through their syndicate

How long should this letter be? Long enough to get you in every publication possible, but short enough to do all its tasks briskly, fully, and—most important—convincingly. A page or two, probably, with attachments, if necessary. Plus those columns. Both must shine. A super letter and lousy columns will be as effective as super columns and a lousy letter. Which do you believe? Make both work and Royko and Bombeck are in big trouble!

CHAPTER 23

Other Cover Letters

PHOTOS AND ILLUSTRATIONS

The discussion of photos and illustrations (drawings, maps, charts, etc.) in this book concerns only those submitted with or supplementary to written copy, such as prints or slides with a travel article, diagrams for a book, or a cover shot in conjunction with an article.

Discussion of other uses and the means of submission of photos are best left to the respective professional fields and their how-to journals of marketing, or to *Photographer's Market.*

In most cases you simply mention their availability in a query letter, indicating the kind, quantity, and perhaps something about the quality of the photos or illustrative materials, and then offer to send the items for the editor's perusal and selection with your manuscript. Sometimes you should describe an item of particular importance or uniqueness in greater detail. Some even send a proof as an example.

Cover letters might be sent about photos or illustrations in two cases:

1. As a paragraph or segment of the cover note or letter (containing comments similar to those in Cover Letter 1) to newspaper travel and simultaneous submission markets, syndicates, or reprint buyers.

2. As a special note to editors buying fillers or with an actual manuscript, previously queried, when it's submitted or if it's delayed. In such a case there would have to be something of unusual worth about the photo or illustration to bring to the editor's attention.

For example, while preparing a piece on *pelota de guante* in Quito, you captured an extraordinary shot of the ball striking a rare bird in flight. Or you have a time sequence showing a patch of forest being destroyed by the flow of lava from a fresh volcano. You took photos of five TV stars while interviewing John Travolta. Or you have access to a photo showing an 800-pound safe being suspended from a coated piece of textile, which you mention in a cover letter that accompanies a filler about a new substance that triples the tensile strength of cloth.

The rationale for the cover letter or note is that the photos or illustrations will make the copy even more valuable to the editor—and yourself.

DELAYED SUBMISSIONS

At times, though rarely, copy requested from a query letter must be submitted after the deadline. In those cases a cover letter is generally required.

Three weeks is the rule-of-thumb submission deadline from the date a query receives a go-ahead. But editors are often more specific, stating an exact date by which the copy must be submitted, sooner if it's urgent, later if its ultimate use is in the more distant future.

Let's say that an editor does give you a three-week deadline. All goes well until your principal interview falls through. Benny Henny has been called to the Upper Xingu to save a collapsing bridge. He won't be back for 10 days, and he is the stanchion supporting your article. Worse yet, the interview could be scheduled only four days before that deadline!

In this case a quick call to the editor is necessary, to explain the dilemma and to ask for a two- or three-week delay in the original schedule.

Then, when you actually submit the manuscript, a cover letter is advisable. In it you remind the editor of the reason for the delay, your phone conversation, and how you believe that the inconvenience actually resulted in a better article, as much as you disliked having to extend the deadline. While you're at it, ask if a sidebar or box would be an interesting insight into how an expert like Mr. Henny solves unusual problems in such distant places on such short notice.

The real purpose of the cover letter with a delayed submission: to remind the editor why the article was delayed. Yet if you can honestly turn that delay, and letter, into a means of expanding your print exposure, great.

Need I say that, as with all writing you display for editors, the cover letter should be topflight prose—well-stated, brief, accurate, and designed to cement in that editor's mind that you can write?

DIRECT SUBMISSIONS

Humor

This is the *Mad Magazine* variety, written to be funny, and unqueriable. What would you say in the query: "Do you want to read something funny?" And what could the editor say back but "Send it to me so I can see if it makes me laugh!"

So common sense says that it should be sent straight in, unadorned and unaccompanied, so you don't draw attention from the laughs.

Yet there can be exceptions. Sometimes it may not be apparent why readers would find the topic interesting, even if it is funny. You know why, so your cover letter informs the editor.

You may be aware of something about to occur that will touch the editor's readers and the reason your humorous piece will be especially timely when published. Your letter tips the editor off.

At times your humor might be even funnier, if that's possible, if you include cartoons or comic illustrations. Even more amazing, if that too is possible, you just happen to know the person who produces those magic laugh-multipliers. Tell the editor, include a few examples, and either give the person's address or offer to provide both the illustrations and the other person's written permission to use them.

These are the most obvious reasons why a cover letter might accompany nonqueried humor. There may be others. But the reasons had better be legitimate. It's best not to detract from the humor with needless add-ons. Useless correspondence will leave you with egg on your face. The yoke will be on you.

Novels

Novels, like short stories, are best sent straight in, without attachments or cover letters, unless it is imperative that the editor know more than he or she can already guess: You want to sell the tome, you wrote it, some of the incidents in the book are based on actual events, and so on.

A few publishers want to read every word, and thus want you to submit the entire manuscript; others prefer sample chapters (often three), sometimes with a synopsis. List the publishing houses selling novels similar to yours. Librarians are your best friends here. Put those publishers in the order in which you want them to consider your book, and follow their instructions on what to send. The book publishers' section in the current *Writer's Market* tells all.

You might send a cover letter with the material in the following cases (and others where it is to your specific advantage):

1. If you've been in print often and impressively. Editors prefer to deal with professionals rather than newcomers—usually. A track record says that you can be depended on to produce what's contracted—usually. And that you'll be more agreeable when it comes to rewrites—usually.

2. If your novel relies heavily on fact. Indicate the primary sources used in compiling those facts and offer to substantiate all critical points, if it's necessary.

3. If your novel talks about actual people, living or dead. Say where you got your information, quotes, and opinions—and how one can verify them should libel be a consideration.

4. If you have expertise in a field that is drawn upon in the novel. Explain your credentials, experience, or whatever the editor should know to be convinced of your understanding of the topic—and offer to prove all claims made, if it's necessary.

5. If your novel is co-authored. Explain that you are representing both yourself and the other author, and indicate or show some signed authorization

to do so, or state that each author must be contacted separately.

6. If the editor must know certain facts or conditions beforehand (that become evident in the unfolding of the text) to understand your novel. Explain them, briefly, so the selected chapters make sense.

7. If your novel concerns a subject about to "explode" on the public, one that will elicit wide public attention (or even more limited but profound interest among a particular group). Mention how you know and when this explosion is likely to occur.

8. If your novel will have particular sales appeal abroad—in a certain country or region—and that isn't apparent. Explain why that is so and how you know.

9. If you have any other information that will help sell your book, should it be published, that the editor and the sales division can't readily guess.

Short Stories

Most editors who buy short stories—a diminishing breed (in number, not size)—simply want to read the stories. If the stories don't work, if they are aimless vignettes or artless ditties or babble inchoate, the editors haven't time to care about the author, the story's background, what is trying to be said, or the rest of it. The material is unusable.

So your first task is to write well, and then find a publication that uses short stories. The next step is to submit your best work. Prayer follows for some. Others call upon patience, vino, or more writing, relying on those much-relied-upon odds to offset editorial insensitivity to the recognition of true genius.

When does the cover letter fit in? Seldom. A direct submission rarely needs an accompanying letter, just a SASE. The editor can see that what is being sent is a short story. Presumably you want to be paid and informed if the gem(s) will be published, returned, or fed to livestock.

A cover letter may be sent if you have sold to that publication before—editors too have lapses of memory, or new editors replace the old. Or if the subject so hinges on the correctness of some specific knowledge and you feel it imperative to tell how you know the facts. Or other details: You are offering a reprint; this is the core story, never sold, from which your current script is being filmed starring Robert Redford and Sonia Braga; this is a translation, now in the public domain, of a piece by Brazil's greatest short story writer, Machado de Assis, and so on.

There are times when cover letters accompany short stories, but those are few and the causes are exceptional. If an editor likes the work and has questions, be certain those will be asked. Just let the editor get to like the story first.

PART FIVE

Common Ground

CHAPTER 24

The Components of a Query or Cover Letter

Q uery and cover letters are business letters, and business letters too often are clean, quick, and bland. You want to change the blandness, particularly in the query. It should display the kind of writing you promise to use in the article: exciting, direct, crisp— the reverse of bland. In both, keep the quick and the clean.

FORMAT

Most business letters use some form of the block format. In the complete block format, all elements, including the heading and the signature block, line up along the left-hand margin.

In the example of a query letter that follows (typical of all query letters I write), I use a modified block form (see Diagram 2). Note the three exceptions from

Diagram 2 Modified Block Letter Form

Return address:
123 Main Street
Santa Maria, CA 93456
(805) 123-4567
Month 1, Year

Inside address:
Mr. Harry Smith
Editor, *The Smith*
5 Beekman Street
New York, NY 10038

Salutation:
Dear Mr. Smith:

_____
_____
_____

_____
_____
_____
_____
_____

_____
_____

Complimentary close:
Sincerely,

(handwritten signature)

Signature identification:

Gordon Burgett

IEC block (initials, enclosures, carbon copies):
GB: cc
Encl.: annotated bibliography
cc: Somebody Else

the full-block format. The return address (in lieu of a letterhead) and the date (both are parts of the heading), as well as the signature block, are lined up along an imaginary line drawn vertically (see Diagram 2). The body of the letter in either form is single-spaced except between paragraphs, which are set off by double-spacing instead of indentation. Spacing of the other elements can be seen in the example.

I follow the same modified form in all full cover letters. Shorter cover notes are simplified, as can be seen in Cover Letter 3 in Appendix B.

PAPER

The stationery commonly used for query and full cover letters is 8½×11" white bond, at least 20 weight or heavier. Avoid using onionskin paper or any other that claims to be erasable. Onionskin paper makes editors weep. It curls up after a few days of handling and later must be pinned down or held flat to be read. It also turns yellow. Erasable paper is simply too much of a good thing. Not only can your thumb erase every word if you're careless in handling it, so can anybody else's simply by touching it. If your typing falls short of perfection, use correction fluid, correction tape, or edit on the computer before printing the text.

Short cover notes, such as those sent for newspaper travel submissions, are prepared on paper specifically trimmed to cover only the top section of the copy. This paper is 8½" wide (or less) and 5¼" long. It has my name, address, and phone number printed at the top (see Cover Letter 1 in Chapter 19).

LETTERHEAD

Do as you wish here. Many writing instructors urge students to rush to the nearest printer to purchase pounds of prepared paper, with matching envelopes, on the assumption, I presume, that if the paper looks impressive and weighty, your query letter will follow suit, and a go-ahead can't be far behind. (Which brings to mind the tale of the farmer who dressed his donkey in pinstripes to make him look like a man—but wound up instead creating two odd-looking asses!)

A query letter does what it aims to do when it prods an editor into asking to see your manuscript. I'm not convinced that letterheads make much difference or that typing your return address connotes anything more than a return address.

Still, if you feel that a letterhead adds needed class to your presentation, or shows more professional commitment, then make the investment. But do draw the line at identifying yourself as Tom Smith, Writer. Or Freelance Writer. Maybe I say this because each time I see it, the person using such stationery can't write wrongs, and the self-proclaimed title makes me laugh. A personal bias, of course. Yet a writer is one who writes—and sells. A name, address, and phone number are sufficient for a letterhead. They should be set in a type size and boldness consistent with a block business letter and quiet enough not to detract from the body of the letter. Letterheads are to identify and impress. If you use one, make sure it does both. If you don't, you still have the body of the query to do the impressing. The body is where the action is.

The same logic prevails for cover letters. What you say and what you are selling will determine the outcome, if the letterhead itself isn't so bizarre that it interferes. The one exception was noted in the last segment: special paper for newspaper travel or short cover notes. And that is for expediency. When you're pumping out a dozen notes to different newspaper editors at one time, it gets mighty tedious having to type your full address, for each. Word processors make it easier. But special paper is better yet.

PARTS OF A LETTER

Heading

If you choose not to use a letterhead, the heading should consist of your return address, phone number, and the date, which follows the phone number one or two spaces below. The separating space is optional. On a letterhead, the date is centered below the printed letterhead.

Don't include your name with your return address, just the number and street name, followed by the city, state (post office two-letter abbreviations are preferred: CA, IL, NY, etc.), and zip code (not separated from the state by a comma). The phone number should include the area code, in parentheses. The date consists of the month written out, the day the letter is written, a comma, and the year. Write out the names of the street, city, and month.

Inside Address

The inside address consists of the name and position of the person to whom you are writing, the name of the publication or publishing house, the address, and the city, state, and zip code.

Why is this information necessary, since you are mailing the letter and the recipient surely knows who and what he or she is? One reason is that you want your query or cover letter to lead to future correspondence—when you send in your copy, when you query again after a successful sale, when they buy reprints, and so on—and it is far easier for you to find this information from your copy of the letter than to have to look up the inside address again each time.

If the person has a title—Professor, Major, Reverend—spell it out, with the exception of Mr., Mrs., Ms., and Dr. If you are certain a woman is married, use Mrs.; if you are uncertain, it is safest to use Ms. With a position title (President, ABC Company; Dean, XYZ College; Secretary, Chamber of Commerce), list the title after the name if it fits on the same line conveniently. If it doesn't, devote a separate line to it, indenting that line if you are using the modified block form.

Don't use periods at the ends of the lines of the inside address unless the last word is an abbreviation (Inc., Corp.). The spelling of the editor's name and the publication should be correct, of course. If you can't take the few seconds required to check both, how can the misnamed soul have much confidence in the factual accuracy of your query or the follow-up article? After all, you already missed the most important fact: the name of the person or firm that you expect to pay your bill!

Salutation

Elsewhere we talk about finding the right recipient for your query letter. Let's assume, for now, that your letter should be sent to Mr. Greg Legg, Managing Editor, *Whippet Star*. Then your salutation would be

"Dear Mr. Legg:". Note the colon. Don't use a comma unless you and Greg are old legg-pulling buddies. (Also omit the quotation marks!)

Since query and cover letters are addressed to one person, should the recipient be unknown to you, don't resort to the aging standby, "Gentlemen:". A gentlewoman may well receive it—not so gently! Make yourself familiar with the publications you write to and find the proper name on the staff list in the most recent issue. Only as a last resort should you direct your letter to a title such as "Editor:" or "Articles Editor:".

Signature Block

The signature block consists of three chips: the complimentary close, the signature, and the signature identification.

The complimentary close is so indiscriminately used it has created a bias in my mind, to the degree that in my query and cover letters I seldom use one at all. Not that I don't want to be congenial or cordial in parting, which is its purpose, but because the standard choices are usually inappropriate and I can't think of a replacement that wouldn't draw undeserved attention to itself.

For example, it is common for editors to wish you "Best!" or "Best wishes!"—often in rejection letters! Which is like praising your arrival while pushing you out the door. Yet if I wish them "Best!" it sounds false.

"Yours truly" is hardly the case, except where it pertains to my copy in exchange for a healthy check. "Respectfully" isn't bad, but it would have a bit more sincerity if I knew them. "Cordially" may be the best of the lot. I'm not certain what "Regards" means in this context, and "Sincerely yours" is true to the point that there is sincerity in what the query or cover says and in my desire to write for the editor for a proper return.

How can I advise you, then, when I have struggled, mildly, with this social artifact, and lost? It may be unimportant which response you use, as long as it's not too bizarre. And it may not count a whit if you use one at all. I sometimes write my name large to fill the space below the text and above my typed signature identification, thinking that a missing complimentary close won't be noticed.

The signature presents no problem at all. Sign the letter in ink under the complimentary close or at a proper distance below the body flush left or along the imaginary vertical line. Don't use a rubber stamp or leave the space blank, unless your intent is to show that you consider the letter unimportant. Also, if your handwriting looks like you are a runaway from a mental ward, or were quietly diplomaed from the third grade, improve your scrawl. The only place on the query letter where your personal mark appears is at the signature. The rest of the letter could read as though it were written by the archangel of journalism, but if your handwriting looks truly moronic, the editor may need just that excuse to say no.

Another thought: You may wish to use only part of your name or another name altogether. See the next chapter for advice on pseudonyms.

The signature identification should appear on the fourth line directly under the complimentary close, or under your written name. It tells who you are, typed so your scrawl can be identified. Don't use "Mr." Women who wish to indicate their marital status may write (Mrs.) or (Miss) before their names, in parentheses.

There is seldom a reason to indicate your position or place of employment, much less to declare yourself a Writer or Freelance Writer. An exception would be if the topic of your proposed article would gain credence if the editor had such knowledge about you. A complex piece describing the newest techniques in brain surgery would be more quickly accepted if your degree, specialization, and institution were mentioned—if they were related to medicine! In such a case, unless these already appear in the letterhead or body of the letter, the degree follows the name; the section or department appears on the next line (if needed); and the company or institution on the line that follows—all single-spaced and aligned under the first letter of the complimentary close.

IEC Block

While an IEC block sounds suspiciously like that clear stuff used on delivery trucks to keep milk cold when I was a kid, the letters actually stand for initials, enclosures, and carbon copies. Technically, they should be included as part of a proper business letter. In queries they seldom are.

The initials (GB:cc, for example) indicate your name (first, in uppercase) and that of the person typing the letter (after the colon, in lowercase). Yet most writers type their own query or cover letters, at least in the beginning, so this can be deleted. (Why fake it if you have no secretary? If the typing is bad, and you still send the letter, it shows poor judgment in keeping the secretary; if it's good, does the editor really care who does the labor?)

The enclosures might be anything from a manuscript to a $100 bribe for the editor to look at your prose. The first is what you are writing the query to avoid, by checking the sense of and need for the article. Logically it can't accompany the query. As for the $100, that would be better spent buying copies of this book for literate friends, or even passersby. (You want editors to pay you, not the other way around.) In other words, unless the enclosures are examples of your printed work, which would surely be mentioned in the letter, you are unlikely to have enclosures with queries.

Cover letters, on the other hand, accompany copy, so in these cases you should note the enclosures. Except with the short cover notes, like those sent to newspaper travel editors. They are stapled or attached directly to the copy, and the paper they are typed on is so short that this formality can be overlooked.

Carbon copies. Or a copy on a computer disk. Of course you make a copy of the query or cover letter for yourself, but you needn't tell the editor that. You'd be thought foolish if you didn't make a copy or told the editor you did. Who else would be interested, or even correctly included, in a business letter between you and an editor? Only in those extremely rare cases when, in fact, a copy of that specific letter is sent elsewhere would you note it. That excludes simultaneous submissions cover notes. The fact that the material is being sent to others will either be noted on the manuscript itself below the word count, or will be mentioned in the cover note itself.

In short, the IEC block probably doesn't appear a few lines below the signature on the margin, flush left, in most query letters because there is nothing to note. It is more likely to be used in cover letters. Our sample letter shows the location and order in which the items should be noted, if they are necessary.

Body of the Letter

The body of the letter is where the action takes place in query and cover letters. Nothing should draw attention away from it.

The body should be error-free, with wide margins and sufficient space at the top and bottom to look balanced. If you must continue on a second page, be certain that at least a few lines of the text carry over, so that the signature block doesn't appear alone.

Some editors refuse to read query or cover letters that can't be presented on one page, assuming that if you can't come to the point quickly in querying or selling printed text, the text itself will be long-winded. One way to limit your letter to one page but offer more information than it will hold is to append attachments: an outline, an opening page of the manuscript, clippings or samples of previously printed work, a bibliographical guide, or other relevant items.

CHAPTER 25

Is a Pseudonym Ever in Order?

New writers sometimes choose to use a pseudonym, or pen name. Legally, that represents no problem unless it is done for fraudulent reasons. But it does have its inconveniences and it can raise doubts.

Try to deposit your check when it is written to the other you without endorsing the real you on the back, unless your account is under the pseudonym—which also has its difficulties.

Or have an editor try to find you when he or she has misplaced your real name and address or phone number.

People you write about or work with may have the same difficulties. And interviewees sometimes feel uneasy about working with a writer who doesn't use his or her own name, as if the use of a pseudonym absolves that writer of responsibility for what he or she writes.

Perhaps the most important point to be made about pseudonyms is that whatever name you use, you are still legally responsible for what you write. And all assets under any of your names are at risk should legal action against you require some payment on your part.

REASONS FOR USING PSEUDONYMS

Then why are pen names used? Novices usually take them for effect, though I fear they end up simply looking affected.

A more substantial reason finds a recognized writer in one genre also writing in another, and, so not to confuse the public image, this writer uses a different pen name in each genre. Publishers sometimes insist on it. A well-known children's writer who is also in print advocating the burning down of courtrooms and the stoning of judges will have two writing names! The deacon of a church who moonlights writing pornography would prefer to have a substitute, rather than a baptized, name in boldface on the racks.

And at times, as we mentioned earlier in a different context, gender connotations may require slight—or total—name alterations, like our woman writing the hockey article for the men's magazine. She either uses her initials or picks a more aggressive, masculine name.

WHY SO MUCH CONCERN OVER THE USE OF A SECOND NAME?

A natural question that others will ask themselves, or you, is why you are using a pseudonym. Editors will be the first to wonder. There is always the thought that if the writer won't let his or her name stand with the research and writing, something must be wrong.

Or that the same article is about to miraculously appear in another publication, and, in a misguided attempt to escape the consequences of improperly selling the same copy twice, the writer has simply changed one authorship.

I'd certainly consider a pseudonym if my name had a foul or misleading connotation in English or in a foreign tongue into which I would be translated. (Fortunately, my surname means nothing internationally but what it says, and it's equally unknown, a fact sure to be rectified when this book hits the stands!)

You may also want to use a pseudonym if the article, when published, puts you or your family in undue danger, or if it compromises you in such a way that using a different name would make sense to the editor. Explain your reasoning to that editor and request that your actual name be, as much as possible, confidential to the publication.

Use a pseudonym if you insist or it's clearly necessary, but be ready to explain why if that use suggests even the slightest touch of impropriety.

CHAPTER 26

Query Letters, Cover Letters, and the IRS

It's a pesky task to properly deduct expenses from your income on Schedule C of your Form 1040 on or before April 15. You must convince the IRS, if you're asked, that your writing is a serious attempt to earn an income—that it's not a hobby.

You may know that and your spouse may know that too, but without repeated sales, a reputation, and a recognized byline, your tax agent won't be so sure.

One way to guarantee acceptance of your deductions is to make a lot of money by writing: the very thing that beginners can't do because they are just getting started. So let's get that acceptance using two other tools: query letters and cover letters.

QUERY LETTERS

Positive replies to query letters are letters of intent. Ideally such a letter of intent would be a written response by the editor on the publication's stationery that says, "I intend to consider, use, and pay you for your manuscript about . . ."

Since that declaration of intent makes the preparation of the manuscript the completion of a business contract (even if the actual payment or amount is not mentioned), all reasonable costs incurred in its preparation are deductible. Those include the paper on which it is written, the stamps and envelope in which it is sent, the typing tool needed to prepare the legible manuscript, the overhead, the costs of acquiring and preparing the information in the manuscript, and much more.

Unfortunately, editors rarely send letters of intent that even vaguely resemble the ideal. Most have probably never heard of the term. Instead they scribble on the top of your query, "Let's see it," and mail it back. *Voila!* That's enough! Any positive reply telling you to prepare the manuscript for serious consideration for publication is considered sufficient, I am told by the IRS.

And what if they don't buy it? You can still deduct all reasonable expenses incurred. The editor responded in good faith; you accepted and followed through on the contract in the same way. Editors generally won't buy until they see the final product: the idea, the words, the finished article. Thus you must produce the manuscript, as promised in the query.

Query letters are the professional's best friend. The written go-aheads are pure tax gold. (Oral go-aheads lack this verifiability. If an editor gives you an oral OK, ask that it be confirmed in writing for your tax records.)

QUERY LETTERS ALSO
CONFIRM WRITING VOLUME

There is a second reason, virtually as strong, why query letters are a tax boon to writers at all levels.

If audited, you will be judged, in the hobby–business determination, by the volume of output you produce each year. If you send off a poem a month or jot a query every quarter, that doesn't speak strongly for your business claim. Too little, too infrequently.

Keep a record of all items mailed and responses received. The number of items recorded or the volume displayed, and the potential income versus the actual costs claimed, will weigh heavily should the IRS attempt to disallow your claims because your writing is a hobby and thus the costs are not deductible.

Query letters are the way professionals sell their skills. Keep a copy of each one you send, plus every reply to prove that in fact the letters were received and responded to. Queries generate go-aheads, and sales generate reprints, rewrites, and other sales. From the volume professionally done and verified comes the right to deduct all reasonably related costs.

COVER LETTERS

Cover letters figure heavily in the volume of potential sales. They are sales letters pure and simple. Instead of being sent to test the market's receptiveness to an idea and an article about it, they attempt to sell items already in existence.

Every cover letter sent, with each item it attempts to sell, should also be listed on your mailing record.

The following section shows a simple way to keep track—and show the tax folk if they ask. Also, keep a copy of every cover letter, with the reply, to verify the volume actually mailed.

KEEP RECORDS AND RECEIPTS

You will be making money by your writing, if you're not already. Keep a tally of all income: amount, date received, and what it is for. That's the fun part.

You must also keep accurate, verifiable records of all expenses. You must be able to prove how much money was spent, when, and how it related to writing if you want to take legal deductions.

If you pay with a check, mark in the lower left-hand corner what it is for. An example might be *Writing: Stamps* on a check to the postmaster. Credit cards are acceptable too, if you keep the receipts or monthly reconciliation sheets and mark a similar notation on each. For individual receipts, also mark each and put it, with the rest, in a box or large envelope for tally at the end of the year. Finally, car costs (other than parking or toll receipts) are usually best claimed on the per-mile basis, so keep a booklet in your glove compartment in which you record—each time the car is used for writing-related purposes—the date, the mileage (or odometer readings), and how that relates to writing.

Here is an example of the last point. Your booklet might read

May 12	19 miles	interview with J. Hill for *Pet Life*
May 14	3 miles	mail query letter
May 15	26 miles	university library for research

KEEP A MAILING RECORD

Your mailing record is as important as your receipts and records, for agents will be as interested in how much money you could have made as how much you spent.

A simple but rigorously kept record will do. Mine notes the year and page number atop each sheet, with about six entries that are separated by an inch or two of space in which I can enter all that transpired relating to that query or submission. To give you an idea, three entries on one page might read like this.

May 15: Q—Ozark banjo player	*Music Journal*
May 16: Fee change at Yosemite	*Chicago Tribune*
May 17: 2nd—Echolocation/whales	*Radar Reader*

A quick explanation. In the first case, the "Q" means a query letter. I'll record all that happens, by date, below it so I know what is taking place and, if necessary, so will Uncle Sam. The second is a simultaneous submission to newspaper travel editors; thus it is a manuscript being sent straight in. And the third is a reprint offer. The article has already been sold, so I'm offering second rights (also called reprint rights) for it to *Radar Reader.* The second and third items will be sent with cover letters, and I'll keep a note of all responses and follow-throughs in the space below the entries.

THE DISCLAIMER—AND ENCOURAGEMENT

Alas, I'm not a tax expert and specific questions should be discussed with the IRS office, a tax accountant, or a lawyer.

But just keep querying and reselling. Keep clear records, copies, and receipts. Keep the faith and keep writing. And keep those deductions that are rightly yours. You earned them.

CHAPTER 27

Some Words About Desperation—and Success

There are times when beginners are so damned mad about their inability to crack into what they see as the publishing "big time" that they grow desperate. Anything can provoke that final break. A friend's negative comments or a spouse's indifference while reading your best work. A three-month delay ended by a mimeographed rejection. Despair creeps in and creates momentary madness.

In the grips of such *locura*, some writers drop to their literary knees and beg an editor to "give them a chance," to "let somebody, anybody, see their work," and so on. They plead that he or she is their last hope (an editor particularly likes to be offered a manuscript last!), and that unless their article is bought, they will quit writing—or worse! If there is a worse.

Sound like a pit into which you might stumble—or leap? Resist. It's simply too desperate, and too final: It ensures defeat. What editor could ever rely on such an unstable writer? Would you put your riches in the hands of a person who came to your door begging and tearing out his hair and wailing that he just had to manage your money?

I have no cure for such desperation, simply advice against it—and compassion, for often I shared those feelings. Maturity includes patience and a reservoir of self-confidence. They are part of the toughness needed to succeed in freelancing.

There's another answer, too, though one I offer with more than mild reluctance. Perhaps you should quit writing, at least for a while. Read or take a few days off to go backpacking or look up old friends or even talk to your mate. Restore some balance to your whole life. List all the things that you do well and are sought by others. Soon enough you will be able to add writing to that list. Often that helps reduce the sense of endless rejection and eternal doom.

No panaceas, no magic cures. Just the certainty that there are ways to sell and ways guaranteed that you won't sell, and operating from a base of defeat ensures the second result.

AND A FINAL WORD ABOUT SUCCESS

Two writing friends made the same suggestion when reviewing this book in its final draft. They felt that the six preceding paragraphs were so depressing they should be left out.

Well, I overruled them because I knew that kind and depth of despair, and I think all new writers experience it. I also kept the information in because I sincerely believe that if you can write at all, and if you put the how-to aspects of this book to the test, you will see positive results soon—and desperation, rather than those paragraphs, will be cast out. (Mind you, despair is tenacious and will try to return. But well-written queries and cover letters will chase it away as surely as garlic will put a vampire to flight!)

One thing is certain. Professionals sell through the use of query and cover letters. This book tells you what those letters are, what they contain, when they are sent, who should receive them, and much, much more. You must find the idea and do the thinking, researching, sorting, writing, and editing. Together we can pull you through that hourglass to get your manuscript seriously considered and bought—then bought again and again. Then desperation will become a sad memory that you will be too busy to contemplate.

You are an important person, more so as a writer because you can share your uniqueness with many people. You put thoughts into words. You bring to others joy and hope and guidance and inspiration, laughter and thought and promise, and in the process you become a wiser person and a better writer.

Yet to be a writer in the complete sense you must be in print, and that requires an uncertain crossing of an indifferent and crowded sea. Query and cover letters are the vessels used by the "old salts." Jump aboard, and bon voyage!

---◆---

If a query does its job, I have a good idea what the article will be like and the chances of its being rejected are almost nil.

> Bill Sonneborn, former
> *editor,* Michiana Magazine
> (South Bend Tribune)

Additional Query Letters— with Comments

Query Letter 4

123 Main Street
Santa Maria, CA 93456
(805) 123-4567
Month 1, Year

Mr. Ted Hanrahan
Editor, *Newspaper Magazine*
10 E. Barker Street
New York, NY 10000

Dear Mr. Hanrahan:

Two bets: (1) that your readers can't name three of the seven kings who ruled in the Americas and (2) that they'd read an article about them, first word to last, if the piece were properly laced with humor, facts, and anecdotes.

Kings sell, particularly this lot: four were white, three black; some were home grown, others came from the oldest European lines; two couldn't read their names if they could write them, one translated Longfellow; one even killed himself with a silver bullet!

Who were they? Three ruled the "gem of the Caribbean," the wealthiest colony in the New World during Napoleon's time: Haiti. Jean-Jacques I (Dessalines) was a butcher of the worst blood yet the first to declare an American independence. The statue in his honor in a Port-au-Prince park is the bust of a Central American despot! Henri I (Christophe), a British free-boy sold into Haitian slavery who helped fight for U.S. independence, was Haiti's greatest king. Faustin I came later. He was picked from a hat, put the hat on his head, and ruled for 11 long, backward years.

Mexico's Agustin I (Iturbide) freed his country from Spanish occupancy, was deposed, and returned once too often. He was no luckier against the firing squad than was Maximilian, who, four decades later, was summarily dispatched to a higher kingdom by Benito Juárez. "Max's" wife went mad and a World War I battle in Belgium was moved a few miles away to avoid disturbing her.

Pedro I, kin to Maximilian (who later fell madly in love with Pedro's tubercular daughter), was a wiry rascal raised in the royal Brazilian stables, issue of an unstable mother and a Portuguese king (João VI) on the lam from Napoleon. Pedro I could master women and horses but couldn't harness his own will. He left his five-year-old son to rule the hemisphere's largest land. Pedro II grew to be 6'4", learned a dozen tongues, ruled for 49 years, and was responsible, in part, for the sudden fame of Alexander Graham Bell at the 1876 Philadelphia Centennial Exhibition.

I've been in print 350-plus times, and will gladly submit on speculation. Are your readers ready for the royal treatment?

Thanks.

Gordon Burgett

Query Letter 4: A General Interest Article for a Sunday Supplement

Lead: first paragraph. Selling a history piece is about as hard as selling an almost dead ox. Worse yet, the people being written about—kings!—aren't even from the United States. So this query letter has to read fast, well, and be particularly fetching. Even then, it is probably going to be rejected.

The idea of "two bets" is to pique the editor's curiosity. Can the editor, much less the readers, name three—or any—of the seven kings of the Americas? Does the editor even know there were kings in the Americas? And would that editor's subscribers read an article to find out more about them? I suggest that those readers will—if the piece is funny, accurate, and full of real-life accounts.

Second paragraph. This paragraph might be eliminated, as I read it with hindsight. Its value is that it shows the variety of people discussed in the piece and, by implication, the breadth of potential interest that variety might have to attract more readers. Kings sell, I tell the editor, as if I know and he doesn't! Black kings, white kings, local grown and imports, some educated, some as dumb as cactus, and just who was it who killed himself with that silver bullet? (Henri I.)

Body of the letter. The next three paragraphs devote a sentence or two to each ruler, capturing some humorous yet true facet of his personality or fate, to make the editor want to read more. It's crucial that these paragraphs read well and that the ideas flow to keep the editor reading and to show that the piece will be written in the same light, tongue-in-cheek fashion. Wordplay is important too, to convey the maximum of both meaning and humor with a minimum of words.

Conclusion. How does the editor know that at that time I had been in print in magazines 350 times? My word only. But the letter looks and reads as if it's written by a professional. I'm not sure the editor cares, frankly. I'll submit on speculation. If the copy doesn't live up to the promise of this query, the editor's not committed. But if I get a go-ahead, I'll produce a top-grade article. Then if this editor doesn't buy it, another will.

Cost

My cost? Three hours in the library, some facts picked up during college studies, an hour with

Writer's Market preparing a market list, and 20 minutes writing the query.

Time Factor

The last king died more than 100 years ago. The topic will keep until the idea is sold many times in different forms. No season is best here, making it an ideal general item for those magazines that print months in advance.

In Retrospect

I'd redo the first and second paragraphs. The first, reading it years later, has a touch of defensiveness to it, a sort of daring the editor, of holding him or her to the wall and shouting a challenge. Or am I imagining that? The second adds little, as is. I'd rewrite it, with more exciting facts—or cut it out completely. The rest is OK. As it is, it worked.

Query Letter 5

> 123 Main Street
> Santa Maria, CA 93456
> (805) 123-4567
> Month 1, Year

Mr. Robert H. Rufa
Managing Editor, *Travel Magazine*
Floral Park, NY 11001

Dear Mr. Rufa:

> Ya got trouble, friend,
> Right here, I say,
> Trouble right here in River City!

River City exists! It's hiding in north-central Iowa much as

Harold Hill described it in Meredith Willson's smash hit *The Music Man.*

The trouble, you recall, was a billiards hall, the Pleazol, and the path to salvation was a marching band— instruments bought sight unseen from the same Harold Hill.

If you go to Mason City today, walk north on Federal Avenue from Central Park, and look down, you will see, in marble for all time: PLEAZOL! Alas, times change. The pool hall has moved four doors away. There's still trouble in River City!

I'd like to take *Travel* readers back to "River City" to see the source of so much fun. Seventy-six trombones still play to tapping feet somewhere in the world every night, 25 years after the musical made its debut!

We'll visit Meredith Willson's hometown, walk the streets and talk with "plain men, modest men," then cross the bridge to see Marion the Librarian's old haunt (now housing Iowa Kempfer Mutual Insurance) or where Marion (Meredith's mother) lived, close to Willow Creek, the "river" of River City.

What's more, since *Travel* pieces include the surrounding area, we'll visit the Hobo Center of America, the "Little Brown Church in the Vale," the site where the 4-H emblem originated, fossil beds throughout the region, a buffalo preserve, the only known habitat of a rare relict mouse, Hamlin Garland's home—the kinds of places one finds in the country Midwest.

I've been in print 350-plus times, in travel, humor, and general interest magazines. I'm not tooting my own horn, just Willson's flute as he did at the Cerro Gordo Hotel for the Kiwanis Club on a Wednesday afternoon in 1912. That's how it all began for him and Mason City.

Interested? I can also provide 24 made-to-order 35mm slides "as pretty as the American flag on the Fourth of July," as Harold Hill would say. A bit corny, but that's Iowa.

Gordon Burgett

Query Letter 5: A Travel Article for a National Magazine

Lead: first paragraph. Instant identity is what your article's lead seeks, and if you can do the same in the query, great. In this case, since the proposal concerns *The Music Man*, the quickest way is to pluck lyrics from the musical. I will have to follow up that reference to trouble later.

Second paragraph. The focus of this piece is Mason City, the model for Willson's River City. And since the lead ends with "River City," the next paragraph picks right up on it. It exists. It's in Iowa. Much as it was described.

Third paragraph. Cite something that proves that Mason City still looks like River City. And bring in that trouble from the lead. What do you have? PLEAZOL, the pool hall.

Fourth paragraph. And there it is, in marble on the main street, PLEAZOL. By giving the precise location I show the editor that I have been there or at least have accurate, precise facts. I also took several photos of that word inscribed in marble, to add visual proof to the statement.

Fifth paragraph. At last, what I am offering: a chance for Rufa's readers to visit, in print, the source of the musical. In other words, an article! I also remind him that, despite the age of the musical, it is still very, very popular. That means his readers will still care about River–Mason City.

Sixth paragraph. A bit more about the town, to show that enough exists to merit an article and that I know enough to write about it.

Seventh paragraph. Here I show that I've at least read the *Writer's Market* write-up of *Travel's* needs, if not the magazine itself. The publication wants a focal point plus information about what its readers can do within a 50-mile radius. So I dig up additional facts to put more flesh on the map. A hobo center and a relict mouse aren't much, but I'm doing the best I can with what's available, folks. Just as you'll have to do. I could tell them that Disneyland is a few miles away, except that it's easier to prove the truth.

Penultimate paragraph. I've worked my credits in, just in case the editor gets shaky with a beginner writing about the sticks. The chance to slip in more background about Willson and Mason City sets up the opportunity to sell my skills. The key thing is to stay centered on the topic and to bring it to life in one page.

Conclusion. An action question: Are you interested? And another chance to zip back to Harold Hill and Iowa while telling the editor that I have 24 good slides of the area.

Form

This letter is long so I had to bend business letter convention. The complimentary close, which I seldom use anyway, was deleted to save space, keep the letter to one page, and leave some white space to balance the presentation physically. I mention it only to emphasize, again, that nothing is sacred except the message.

In Retrospect

This is one of my favorite query examples because it never strays from the topic. There's something else too.

By reading the query do you think I've already been to Mason City? Good, I want you to think I'm on top of the subject. But I never said I'd been there, nor would that make much sense. I hadn't been close. Only the comment about the photos could be misleading—but I can provide them, after I take them when I visit the site!

The query's contents came from several hours of library work, phone calls to Mason City, reading a copy of the script, and studying a map to list other interesting sites and features nearby. (The entire process forms the core of *How to Sell More Than 75% of Your Freelance Writing*.) Add to the hustle a bit of common sense, some tight editing, and this query received a quick go-ahead, which in turn produced an article (with a cover photo) that ultimately repaid itself 10 times over the original check.

Query Letter 6

123 Main Street
Santa Maria, CA 93456
(805) 123-4567
Month 1, Year

Mr. Jon Larsen
Editor, *The Runner*
1 Park Avenue
New York, NY 10016

Dear Mr. Larsen:

Running's least likely record holder has to be 96-pound Margaret Miller, a 52-year-old Sears saleslady from Thousand Oaks, California.

For one thing, she is hypoglycemic and must follow a diet almost the reverse of her competitors. For another, until 10 years ago the highlight of her life was being chosen a Highland dancer in her hometown of Glasgow, Scotland.

Now Margaret holds the world record in both the mile and the marathon—for females 50 and over. Last week she set the distance record for her class for the one-hour run. When will it end?

I met Margaret when she parked in front of me at a 10K in Ventura, California, and later when we finished seconds apart. We shared some tea and words, and when I undiplomatically pried her age from her, I asked how many women her age could beat her. "None," she half-whispered, and the truth slowly emerged.

Must it emerge that slowly for *The Runner*'s new readers? I'd like to share the "why's" of a 50-plus female who made a dramatic change in her life a decade back, and who will enter her first Boston Marathon this April, a lass who runs 55 miles a week between grandmothering, working, and nursing a running husband.

My writing background is on better footing than my own weekend running: 350-plus items in print—tearsheets or copies gladly sent. Yet since I work on speculation, and sell better than 90% of that, what I need is a go-ahead, a copy of your new publication, and any length suggestion you wish to share.

Please let me know. Thanks.

Gordon Burgett

Query Letter 7

123 Main Street
Santa Maria, CA 93456
(805) 123-4567
Month 1, Year

Mr. Richard B. Stolley
Editor, *People Weekly*
Time-Life Building
Rockefeller Center
New York, NY 10020

Dear Mr. Stolley:

Margaret Miller is indeed likely to have been missed by
one of your West Coast stringers. In fact, I might not have
found her either had we not all but literally crossed paths
in Ventura, California, in a 6.2-mile race last Sunday!

Who is she? Margaret holds both the mile and marathon
record—for women 50 and over! Which, 10 years back,
would have shocked her neighbors in Thousand Oaks
because the former Scottish Highland dancer had never
even run. Even today few of her co-workers at Sears know
of this petite lass's long-run excellence. A grandmother at
52, Margaret wages a daily battle against hypoglycemia
and follows a diet so severe that she can't even
"carbohydrate-pack," which is the marathoner's way of
storing energy for a long race. Instead, she sips cider,
loosens her legs, and heads across the countryside, training
at precisely 55 miles a week, and winning within minutes
of her estimated goal.

In December, in San Pedro, California, she will attempt to
better her own record for the third time. That might be an
ideal date peg for publication, if the idea interests you.

My background includes 350-plus items in print—
tearsheets or copies of recent titles gladly sent.

Are you ready for a biography, a question-answer interview,
or anything else about this latter-day, 96-pound dynamo
whose special kind of courage and joy sprung from utter

despair only a decade back when, for more reasons than one, she began running for her life?

Please let me know. And thanks.

Gordon Burgett

Query Letter 8

123 Main Street
Santa Maria, CA 93456
(805) 123-4567
Month 1, Year

Mr. James Wiggins
Executive Editor
Dynamic Years
215 Long Beach Boulevard
Long Beach, CA 90802

Dear Mr. Wiggins:

Having taken on and conquered the gray whales, I have an even more exciting story for you: the gray marathoners!

The center of my query is a former Highland dancer turned world-record holder in both the marathon and the mile—for women 50 and over. Margaret Miller is a 52-year-old Sears saleslady, grandmother, and hypoglycemic of Thousand Oaks, whose 96-pound frame was as far from athletic excellence 10 years back as her mind was from happiness.

How she brought her life into balance and went on to set a handful of world running records might be the focus. Or Margaret as one of the emerging matrons of the long run, with the focus on the 50-plus runners in the world today, male and female.

Two time factors are worth considering. In December she will attempt to better her marathon record for the third time, in San Pedro. And next April she will enter her first

Boston Marathon, if injuries don't interfere. The Boston event might be a particularly good publication target, allowing me to expand the piece to include other older runners who will be competing in running's most prestigious distance race.

We first met while competing in a 6.2-miler in Ventura, running side by side the entire way! We've spoken for hours since, I've made the usual cross-checks for truth, and what has emerged is a story any reader would enjoy, full of spunk, laughter, courage, and a special kind of joy from a lass who turned to running in sheer despair.

Are we to team up again to delight your readers?

Thanks.

Gordon Burgett

Query Letters 6–8: The Same Subject Queried Simultaneously to Three National Publications

Article ideas are like fallen leaves, everywhere for the picking. Take the sunny morning of August 5, 1978, when I was parking my car before running in a 6.2-mile race in Ventura, California. A petite woman about 50 years old, in running shorts and a singlet, emerged from a VW in front of me and we exchanged "good days" en route to the sign-up table.

Later, much to my surprise, I found myself racing the same tiny form to the finish line! On the way back to our cars we exchanged the usual runners' talk. She was extremely soft-spoken and modest. It was all I could do to find out how a grandmotherly waif could chug up and down hills and skim the beachfront at a sub-seven-minute-mile pace. With much prodding the truth finally emerged: Margaret Miller, a Scottish transplant, wasn't an everyday jogger. She held both the American mile and world marathon records for women 50 and over!

That night I prepared a writing plan to sell articles about my newfound topic. I would phone *Runner's World* to confirm that she did hold both records, interview Margaret by phone to pick up the essential biographical facts needed for a query, read up a bit on women's long-distance running to put their times and ages into perspective, and then send query letters to an assortment of publishing markets.

Which markets would be interested in buying a story about a California grandmother who simultaneously held two of the most demanding running records? Surely a running magazine, and probably one from the women's market, a California publication (perhaps in-flight or regional), a retirement monthly, and perhaps some other, more general magazine.

Runner's World confirmed Miller's ranking, plus added another she held for her age: the one-hour distance record. Margaret turned out to be as warm and sharing during the phone interview as she was fast on the track. Even better, the preliminary interview yielded enough personal information to impart a sense of depth and intimacy to the query. Most important, she was flattered at the prospect of an article and showed every desire to cooperate with a more complete in-person interview and photographic session later.

Thus, with a $2 phone call to Mountain View and another $3.50 in calls to the Miller home, plus some hours in the library digesting the few tomes about female runners and records, I was ready to write one query that would serve as the base for other queries to noncompetitive markets.

Query Letter 6: *The Runner*

Background. A new national running publication called *The Runner* was about to appear in New York. Since *Runner's World* had just printed a short bio about Carol Cartwright, Miller's closest competitor (and subsequent record-setter in the marathon), it was unlikely that they'd use material so similar again. So I aimed for the new magazine, uncertain of its format but counting on it to have a shortage of West Coast material at the outset.

Salutation. I saw Jon Larsen's name mentioned as the probable editor and knew that *New Times* (since folded), which he had edited, was published by the same house. So I mailed the query to him at the *New Times* address, and hoped.

Body of the letter. Larsen doesn't know Margaret Miller or why he or his readers should, so my key task in the query is to flesh her out and make him want to know her better. Still, his readers are runners; their interests are running and other runners. Many are women; all are aging. Some (horrors!) are even approaching 50. So I emphasize the biographical facts that make Margaret both similar to the readers and still different: a Sears saleslady but from Scotland; 96 pounds, 52 years old, hypoglycemic (and why that matters to a runner); the world's fastest in her class; her modesty about her records yet her courage in entering the Boston Marathon; a grandmother who runs 55 miles a week, and so on. . . .

Fourth paragraph. This one shows that I know her personally and won't be pasting together a secondhand rewrite, or worse. And that I run and am familiar with the technical terms and jargon *The Runner*'s readers know, use, and expect to read.

Conclusion. Simply, I'm a professional and so confident that they will buy my copy I'm not asking for an advance or guarantee before I research and write. (Larsen doesn't know me anyway and probably wouldn't buy outright without seeing some evidence of my work.) I go a step further, saying that I'll submit on speculation so he can see that the work is the caliber he wants. He's got the cards. No time for bluffing. Just play your best hand, which is a good query followed by copy as good or better. It evens out later, when you've sold him some super articles.

Another point: I normally wouldn't query a magazine I hadn't read. If I did violate that rule, I certainly wouldn't let the queried editor know! But in this case *The Runner* wasn't even on the stands, so asking for a copy was proper. In fact, it was imperative, to see what it was printing, how it handled personality pieces, its article layout and lengths, and the level and style of its photography.

Time Factor

Projecting six months from the query date (to allow for manuscript preparation/pix and an estimated three-month lead time the magazine needs to work the material into the edition) puts us into April, the month of the Boston Marathon. This is an ideal release time since Miller would be running her first that same month.

In Retrospect

The letter was somewhat choppy, but it piqued the curiosity of the then managing editor, Marc Bloom:

"Margaret Miller sounds like a fine subject for our People column—not only her running and all that entails but her dancing and other interesting aspects of her life."

Query Letter 7: *People Weekly*

Background. If you send the same query letter about the same idea to many publications at the same time, you might be faced with a lovely dilemma: They might all say yes!

First, you shouldn't send the same query to more than one. Each should be written to sell the idea to a different set of readers, and thus each requires a different approach to the respective editors. True, many—even most—of the same facts would appear in the queries, but the promise—what each article would be about—must differ.

Second, you must write the letters in such a way that even if all the editors say yes, you can prepare manuscripts so clearly different that no editor can complain. In the manuscript just avoid using the same structure, similar leads or conclusions, identical quotes, and many of the same anecdotes.

Comparing the first query to *The Runner* about Margaret Miller with that of *People Weekly,* you will see the major changes in the first and fifth paragraphs, though there are subtle differences throughout. Let's review the *People Weekly* query item by item.

Lead: first paragraph. The then current *Writer's Market* indicated that *People Weekly* wanted subjects who were likely to be missed by its stringers. So the opening line restates that, adding that I too almost missed Margaret Miller.

Second paragraph. Margaret who? This is where she must become human: why she should appear on his pages and why the readers would like to know more about her. Since the editor of a general magazine probably knows less about running than the editor of *The Runner*, I explain in greater detail what hypoglycemia means to a marathoner, and what carbohydrate-packing is. You will notice that in this letter and the next, a 10K race becomes a 6.2-mile race.

Third paragraph. *People Weekly* is just that, a weekly, so it needs a date peg, a reason for an article to appear when it does. Here I give one: In December, Margaret will once again attempt to better her record.

Fourth paragraph. In the *Writer's Market* of that year, *People Weekly* requested biographies, question-answer interviews, and shorts, so I suggest that "this latter-day, 96-pound dynamo" might be the subject of any of the three.

Conclusion. I like to end queries with some spur to action on the editor's part, at least to let him or her know what I expect. "Please let me know" is a modest request. Finally, despite what business letter writers say, it never hurts to thank people, or so my mother told me. Thanks, Mom.

If Both Publications Say Yes?

I would focus heavily on Margaret's running, records, and times, with her other virtues woven in, for *The Runner*, and concentrate on the "whole Margaret" for the general piece in *People Weekly*. The leads, pix, quotes, conclusions, and anecdotes should be different, which means more work for me. More interviewing, more quotes, more facts—and two checks.

In Retrospect

I might not have told enough about Margaret. Perhaps another paragraph or two, with some quotes or an anecdote, would have made her more alive. That might have stretched the query to two pages, which has drawbacks. Who knows? You do what you can to get the sale. If you get a go-ahead to one of the three, great. It'll probably be closer to one in seven in the beginning.

Query Letter 8: *Dynamic Years*

Background. The more queries you write about the same subject, the more important it is for you to change the focus of the proposed article. The third query, to *Dynamic Years*, suggests three possible ideas and two target dates. Yet it is the readership of *Dynamic Years* that provides the unique approach to the contents: They are the first post-50 group anticipating or already enjoying retirement.

Lead: first paragraph. I had just sold them an article about whales, and I like to follow up a sale with a query soon afterward, so my name stays fresh. I mention the whales in the query's lead and tie it to marathoning.

Second paragraph. Nothing's new here. I use the same facts from the other queries except that I bunch together her age category, her age, and the fact that she is a grandmother—all near the top of the query because these are of particular interest to *Dynamic Years*.

Third paragraph. I suggest two approaches or slants to the topic: Margaret herself or Margaret as one of the many 50-plus runners of both sexes in the world today.

Fourth paragraph. Time factors are mentioned, plus another slant. If he needs the piece soon, I can include the December record, if it's broken. But if he wants to wait until after the Boston Marathon, she might be more newsworthy and the photos broader in subject. That adds another angle: the older runners at the Boston Marathon.

Sixth paragraph. We teamed up before, I remind him, so why not again?

In Retrospect

Not bad. I might say more about Margaret.

If All Three Say Yes?

Back up the money truck!

Query Letter 9

123 Main Street
Santa Maria, CA 93456
(805) 123-4567
Month 1, Year

Juvenile Editor
Random House, Inc.
201 E. 50th Street
New York, NY 10022

Dear Juvenile Editor:

Chewing gum in the stacks of America's libraries? Bubble Delight oozing from every page of a book? A librarian's curse—unless it's from Random House's fun, fact-filled cartoon/copy book about the history of gum called *The Chicle Kid.*

No, I haven't got my tongue in my cheek. It's that much maligned substance first introduced into the United States by the victor of the Alamo, a former President of Mexico who was trying to earn his way back home by hawking a rubber substitute. Worse yet, the first man to sell gum in volume was a dentist! Cavemen chewed it, Mayans made rain shoes from it, and girls popularized it as a substitute for "chawin' tobacker." By the end of World War II, it was the best-known currency on the globe.

Enclosed are the first 10 pages of a total 48, with cartoons drawn by Larry Litsinger. The prose and illustrations are offered together or separately.

Two of my degrees are in history. More than 350 of my writings have appeared in print. And I was in the sixth grade, with seven cavities, before I became—to avoid parental persecution—a close-lipped chewer.

If the sample sets your mouth to watering, let me know quickly: The rest of the tome will be in the next mail. *The Chicle Kid* is eager to make some publisher rich. He's chomping at the bit.

Is Random House ready to bite off something it can chew with a smile?

Thanks.

                                        Gordon Burgett

Query Letter 9: A Juvenile Book for a Book Publisher

Attachment. Ten pages of a 48-page juvenile booklet accompanied the letter, so the reason for and composition of the query in this case changes considerably. When a query is sent alone, the editor judges you by its content and composition, unless that editor knows you from an earlier contact. In this case, the query is as much a cover letter as a query, and it is less important as a sole selling tool. The first item the editor will consider is the actual copy—the sample pages of the booklet. Only a letter in astonishingly bad taste or one that raises serious doubts about your authorship of the copy would dampen the editor's enthusiasm to see more of a good book.

Lead: first paragraph. In light of the above, it might seem prudent to write a three-line cover note simply telling the editor what is being sent, what I am selling (prose and illustrations together or separately), and what I have waiting to send if the editor is interested. I can't argue with that logic; it might sell. And if the editor is close-lipped about more than gum chewing—that is, if he or she has no sense of humor—indeed this letter may get the project set aside before it's ever really considered.

Yet the booklet is funny and the cartoons funnier. A somber editor wouldn't buy it anyway. So the letter may show that I can write humorously in more than gum books, and it should at least hint at items in other sections of the book that the editor doesn't have in hand, as well as contain the one-paragraph mini-biography. Since this is as much a cover letter as a query, it must be short. So why not write a fun, fact-filled, and to the point letter—like the booklet?

Who shudders most at the thought of chewing gum? Librarians, school teachers, and dentists. So we play on the fears of the librarians in the lead. Publishers are particularly aware of librarians: They buy books. We face that concern, straight on and with humor, that the librarian may reject a book about gum.

Mentioning the company receiving your query in

the lead isn't a bad idea either. Since I don't have a name of a specific editor, tying in the company personalizes the letter a bit. It can't hurt to wed your book with their name, lovingly.

Second paragraph. The history of gum? Why not highlight a few facts and humorous oddities to remind the editor that even gum can have a history sufficiently noble to have been jawed about since people hid in caves?

Third paragraph. Business, quick and plain. The editor may want every book to contain at least 66 pages—or 366. There's a risk in noting that the book is 48 pages long. Yet a clever editor will discover its length soon enough anyway, and by stating it you now have a basis for dickering. It can be stretched to 66! (But 366?) It's also important that the editor know that you aren't the illustrator's Siamese twin—that the copy and the cartoons can be bought separately or together.

Fourth paragraph. The simplest of biographies—of me. I wrote the prose; I'm selling the book. The editor will probably have a house artist for illustrations. If Larry's work is chosen, great; I'll fill him in later. In three sentences the editor knows that I have more than two degrees (can probably read and write), two are in history (so I might be able to tell a fact from a fiction), I've managed to bribe or woo editors at least 350 times to put an item of mine in print (either expect a bribe or good writing), and that at least in the sixth grade, when I had all of my teeth, I had first-hand experience with the substance in question.

Conclusion. More of the same malarky—but not

madness. If you want more, I say, I'll send you the rest. It's done and ready to go. Not a tease. The book has been written and illustrated; you can see it in a week. And I think it will make somebody money, besides me.

In Retrospect

It's a good query–cover letter, fast and to the point, setting the editor up humorously to leap into the hilarity of the booklet. Even if the editor printed a gum book last week and swore on a stack of copyright forms to resist such sticky matters forever, the letter says "writer" and "humorist." Maybe that editor has been waiting for just that combination to turn out the definitive work on armadillos. The query shows me to be the ideal person to pen that specialty. After all, if I can write about gum . . . So instead of replying to me, "No, get lost," the reply may be "No, not this time, but you might be interested in . . ." I'd have to be terribly hard-shelled to refuse.

Query Letter 10

123 Main Street
Santa Maria, CA 93456
(805) 123-4567
Month 1, Year

Ms. Linda Cammack
Articles Editor, *Fun Abroad*
88 W. 33rd Street
New York, NY 10000

Dear Ms. Cammack:

In mid-December I will again be headed for England and Wales, and I'd like to prepare two articles for you when I return.

The first, for use a year hence in your holiday or December issue, would be "Seeing London for Christmas." I could have it to you, with slides or b/w prints, any time after February 1, should that deadline be particularly early.

London is truly lovely for the holidays—but people must know where to go and how to apportion their time. For one thing, three holidays in a week (Christmas, Boxing Day, and New Year's) make museum visiting and sightseeing difficult, and shopping hectic and spotty. To offset that, it's easier to get theater tickets, parties abound, pubs hum with excitement, and many tourist sites do remain open, to be enjoyed casually without the crowds. Plus there's an added attraction: uncrowded trains to Dover, the Hovercraft to Boulogne—and a wonderful day (or several) in France.

It is precisely that which I'd research this winter to prepare the best action guide for the year to come, taking photos now and updating the details, if you wish, next fall right before final print time. The article will be full of visuals, quotes, anecdotes, some seasonal lore of England, and—most important—it'll be accurate.

The second piece might be for use in the summer. It might be called "The Beaches of Wales," where many of the English enjoy their holidays. Wales is a land of castles, pubs with song, choruses, forts, forests, pride, and inns. And, of course, the visiting English, who in themselves are a delight to see and hear.

I was there last summer, briefly, but will return this winter for 10 days to complete the research and supplement, if nature permits, some shots of the castles. In the process I hope to add to my store of interesting facts and insights what's "best" to see and do, where to stay, and when one should make reservations. Thus it could be a summer story, as suggested, or a March piece about summering in Wales. The choice is yours. I could have the copy and pix in your hands by January 20.

For years I wrote about travel in the Midwest, with some 200 articles in print and twice as many newspaper items. In the past few years I've tried to visit Europe annually and have usually touched London and Wales each time. I'd like

> to share the loveliness of each with those seeking beauty in *Fun Abroad.*
>
> Please let me know in the SASE soon so I can make my on-site plans accordingly.
>
>   Gordon Burgett

Query Letter 10: Pretrip Travel Query Letter

Lead: first paragraph. This says it all: I'm going on a trip and want to know if I should gather information there for later stories for your readers. It tells when and where. Your query can be sent as early as six months before the trip.

Second paragraph. Now you tell the editor when you will be back, by implication here (early or mid-January, to give yourself time to write good copy and get the photos developed), and, more important, when the copy will be in her hands. Since many magazines prepare their Christmas or holiday issue as early as March of the preceding year, this shows professional savvy. The worst the editor can say, other than no, is that she doesn't need it until later.

Third paragraph. Here you show why the trip this year will produce a super article for the following Christmas. It sounds as if you already know London and are particularly conscientious about accuracy—a fastidiousness editors love. There's plenty of spunk and fun promised too.

Fourth paragraph. More of the same. It's good to note that you'll update the facts later. A quick call to the

British travel board, in the United States if you have a few days, in London if not, will get the details adjusted.

Fifth paragraph. I generally limit each query to one idea to give it a full-page sales treatment, but this one, as you see, is an exception. As long as I'll be there and want to see Wales, why not ask for a go-ahead on a beach piece?

Sixth paragraph. You'll note that the paragraphs in my query are short, much as my copy will be, rarely more than three sentences long, usually one or two. Show by example how the writing can be expected to look.

Here I zero in on one story but from two different angles: It's all a beach piece, but either to be run during the summer or in the spring about the summer, so people who want to visit those same Welsh beaches will have time to make arrangements. I let the editor tell me which and promise a quick manuscript if she will use it in the spring. I don't ask if she wants an article, but which one. An ancient sales trick, but I am selling, aren't I? And what a prize she'll win if she says yes: electric prose, radiant verbs, azure nouns, joy with a splash!

Seventh paragraph. A bit about my background—and why I am the person to cover London and Wales.

Eighth paragraph. A simple request which gently reminds Ms. Cammack that I will be doing the work for someone, and I must know for whom and which readers before I leave.

In Retrospect

Somewhat skimpy on the details about both articles, which confirms my prejudice against trying to squeeze two queries onto one page. Yet it may work. Both are legitimate topics—London off-season, and Wales, off the track. And it makes sense to do the legwork for both at the same time, unless she knows that London at Christmas is wet and drab and the beaches in Wales feel like a drizzly tundra come January. If she gives me the go-ahead, I'll put on my union suit and get the facts. The readers will be none the wiser!

APPENDIX B

Additional Cover Letters— with Comments

Cover Letter 3

Gordon Burgett
123 Main Street
Santa Maria, CA 93456
(805) 123-4567
Month 1, Year

Dear Mr. Rosenberg:

"The Land of the Music Man" is a tree-lined Main Street in an Iowa town called Mason City, where Meredith Willson grew up, was raised by "Marion the Librarian," played pool at Pleazol (with its name still in marble on the sidewalk), and walked to school over a bridge that was later immortalized by the musical/movie. The article attached tells what Washingtonians would find today, unchanged, in the setting should they head west for a visit. . . .

I have 16 good-to-excellent b/w's available to select from, if you're interested—or I can send the five best.

Please don't return the ms, just your verdict in the SASE.

Thanks.

Gordon Burgett

Cover Letter 3: Simultaneous Submission Cover Letter

Purpose. This cover note will be read by the editor, enchant him, draw his eyes to the first paragraph of the copy, and pull him through to the last throbbing word on page six, eight, or whatever. Therefore it is stapled prominently on the upper left-hand corner of the front of the first page. Other copies of the same manuscript are being sent to other newspapers that do not overlap in circulation, each with its own note.

Form. The return address includes my phone number, on the long shot that the editor wants to call me to arrange a million-dollar deal. Or get the photos pronto. The note is short and quick, outlines the article in the first paragraph, talks of photos in the second, begs a verdict in the third, and lets those eager eyes dance on to my magnetic wordplay in the manuscript.

Attention. This is sent to the editor of *The Washington Post,* so it talks about Washingtonians and of going west to reach Iowa. Change the tie-ins in each note or you'll have the travel editor of the *Los Angeles Times* with the wrong name and his or her readers heading through China to reach Mason City!

In Retrospect

This was one of my most successful travel submissions, and the note didn't hurt. It makes you want to read more. Just enough tease to do the trick. But then you must have a good manuscript attached. Nobody, not even the most desperate editor, buys these little notes! But a lot will read the manuscripts if the notes pique their interest, and that, folks, is what it's all about.

Another Point

You have read about Mason City already. In an earlier query letter to *Travel Magazine,* you saw this idea first being offered for print. By the time this note was written, the magazine article had appeared and two reprints had already been sold. At this point, the same material is again being rewritten, in a shorter version, and is being offered to newspaper travel editors.

Cover Letter 4

123 Main Street
Santa Maria, CA 93456
(805) 123-4567
Month 1, Year

Ms. Thelma Schooler
Managing Editor, *Women's Reader*
1683 Wilbraham Avenue
Lynchburg, VA 20000

Dear Ms. Schooler:

"River City, USA," the setting of Meredith Willson's
beloved musical, *The Music Man*, could be anywhere the
audience imagined, from Virginia to Montana. It was a
mythical place of marching bands, Harold Hill, Marion the
Librarian, and all the nostalgia of 1912 as vibrant and
young as home-stirred ice cream on the Fourth of July!

But do your readers know that there really was a River
City? And that many of the places woven into fantasy
really exist, like Pleazol, the pool hall, and the bridge over
the river where the movie band marched and played
"Seventy-Six Trombones," and the library and the city
park?

Where is "River City" and what's it like? That's the article
I'd like to share with *Women's Reader*—the city itself,
what visitors to it can see of the musical and Meredith's
life there, what the residents think of their fame (or is it
notoriety?), and how your readers could enjoy, in person,
what we can first let them enjoy on paper.

It's really Mason City, Iowa, as the article attached, from
Travel Magazine, reveals. They purchased first rights and
used the piece in July 1974. I'm offering you second rights,
Ms. Schooler, plus an assortment of forty 35mm slides (as
well as the shots you see in the article) for your selection.

I'll gladly add any of three sidebars to bring the story more
directly to your readership: (1) a detailed list of events in
and near Mason City during the month, and the following
two, that you plan to use the piece; (2) an interview with

Mrs. Adele Lindune, the last of Meredith Willson's teachers still living, with humorous recollections of him and the town, and/or (3) a collection of interviews from women on how the town has changed because of the movie and musical.

If the article (and sidebars—indicate which) interests you, I'll gladly send the original manuscript, the new sidebars, and as many slides as you wish to review. Simply let me know in the enclosed SASE.

The Music Man is America's favorite. Although I've been in print 400-plus times, the enclosed article shows all. If we can team up to delight your readers, great!

Gordon Burgett

Cover Letter 4: Reprint Simultaneous Submission Letter for a Travel Article

Purpose. Earlier in this book we read a query letter offering to write an article about Mason City, site of "River City, USA" in *The Music Man*. At this point that query received a go-ahead, the article was written, and it appeared in *Travel Magazine*, which bought first rights. So we are writing a letter (one of many like it, each adjusted to its respective publication) to see if *Women's Reader* would be interested in using the very same piece, or a modification, as a reprint.

Lead: first paragraph. Thelma Schooler has never been approached about this piece before, so we must sell her in the opening paragraph.

Second paragraph. More of the same: What's this letter and the attachment about? It's harder to sell a reprint, so this cover letter needs all the care you'd put into a query.

Third paragraph. Now we tie it to why the *Women's Reader* would be interested, though in truth it is a general article no more directed to women than men.

Fourth paragraph. Our legal obligations: I'm offering a reprint (as if Ms. Schooler couldn't guess from the copy of the article enclosed!), where it appeared first, when, what rights were bought, and what else I have to sweeten the deal. Slides!

Fifth paragraph. Thelma's thinking to herself, why do I want to use that old piece everybody has already read? So here I suggest three ways that we can put a new dress on a known body, two of them women-oriented! On the other hand, she may think her readers have never seen *Travel Magazine* and would like to use the original unadorned. So I give her four choices, plus photos. Her lucky day!

Sixth paragraph. I mention two things here. One, let me know if she's interested. Two, Thelma may be of saintly stock, but I want to keep tabs on her if she is thinking of using my prose gratis. Her typesetter will want it double-spaced (like the original manuscript), so I offer to send that to her, if she's interested. If she requests it, I will watch future issues of *Women's Reader*. If my gilded words see print, I see flakes of gold.

Finale. Why would any editor buy this piece? It's about America's favorite musical and I wrote it! Be positive but not oppressive.

Cover Letter 5

123 Main Street
Santa Maria, CA 93456
(805) 123-4567
Month 1, Year

Dr. Albert Allaback
Editor, *Marathon World*
654 Fifth Avenue
New York, NY 10000

Dear Dr. Allaback:

The "Three-Peak Marathon" falls about 26 miles short of
the mass appeal of the Boston or the Big Apple. It's
nowhere near as tough as the Pike's Peak horror nor as
grueling as the Western 100. But it has its own cruel sort
of charm that any true marathoner would love!

For one thing, it covers some of America's loveliest terrain,
though it's seen either climbing or descending. The race
leaves Ojai, setting of "The Six Million Dollar Man" and
the earlier film site for "Shangri-La," up a six-mile, 1,300-
foot ascent past Lake Casitas, where Olympic rowing was
held.

Eight miles down to sea level, past lemon and avocado
groves, a twisting mountain road leads the runners to a
seemingly vertical 1.3-mile rise to the peak of Shepherd's
Mesa, which the runners circle in a sea-view aerie of
pastoral calm, in sight of José Ferrer's ranch, and then back
down to sea level. Too soon, at 23.5 miles, the last test of
the true runner's dedication comes in the form of a steep
0.7-mile rise, past Dame Judith Anderson's former
mansion, to the idyllic groves of Cate School. From then
on it's downhill to the California coastal town of
Carpinteria, a few miles south of President Reagan's
summer White House.

Why would any sane human undertake this vertical
torture? And why in backlands California, far from the
maddening crowds? The enclosed article tells all, as it did
to the readers of *Coastal Trails* in January of this year. I'm

offering reprint rights to your readership, 99% of whom probably live outside the other magazine's circulation.

I have available a wide assortment of top-quality slides and b/w prints of the past three marathons—all held on cool, sunny days. Let me know your preference, and I'll send you a choice of the best.

Finally, it's hard to typeset copy using a clipping like the enclosed. If you'd like the original manuscript, for your typesetter's peace of mind if not eyesight, just let me know.

The "Three-Peak Marathon" is held in January when much of the rest of America is knee deep in snow, so it makes ideal midwinter copy. I can update the piece to include any details about the coming event (and notables scheduled to run) if it's used before the race, or I can give an account of the latest actual run, if it's used after.

It's not the big time but it's one of the toughest, and surely among the loveliest, races anywhere in America. Something drew back 62% of last year's participants for a second time! In fact it's the best of both worlds: excruciating and delightful!

Should we share it with the readers of *Marathon World*?

Gordon Burgett

Cover Letter 5: Reprint Simultaneous Submission Letter for a Sports Article

Purpose. This letter covers different ground in almost the same way the previous reprint letter did, so let me zero in on the few novelties in this write-up. The purpose is identical: to sell an article that has already been shared with the general public, in this case about a mythical marathon over actual terrain in a supposed running journal called *Coastal Trails*.

First three paragraphs. Tell why *Marathon World* needs this article, with as much legitimate scene painting and name dropping as possible. I'm certain that a runner scaling Shepherd's Mesa after topping the peaks from Ojai could not care less if a home along the route is owned by Judith Anderson or a hobo, frankly. But it adds visual appeal to the letter— and it's true.

Fourth paragraph. The legal obligation again, plus the fact that almost none of the *Marathon World* readers read *Coastal Trails,* which is important to Dr. Allaback.

The rest. Three things make the piece more appealing: (1) The marathon is run in the dead of winter, when live race copy is hard to find; (2) I can write it before the race, highlighting the event to come (with details about it) but focusing on facts and photos of past runs; or (3) I can zip material about the actual run to the editor as quickly as I catch my breath and get the words on paper. The last two offer a different manuscript from the one already in print.

In Retrospect

It might just be the offbeat, out-of-the-norm piece that a large running publication will use, even as a reprint. Since it has already made money, what have I—or you—got to lose in trying to build on it again and again?

Cover Letter 6

123 Main Street
Santa Maria, CA 93456
(805) 123-4567
Month 1, Year

Mr. Greg Kelsey
Editor, World News Syndication
4444 Fifth Avenue
New York, NY 10000

Dear Mr. Kelsey:

The three enclosed articles about the Amazon should find interested readers abroad, thus I am sending them to you for placement outside North America. (I am still selling reprints of all three in the United States and Canada, however.)

The first, "Gold in the Oriente!," is a first-person adventure about a gold hunt I led up the headwaters of the Amazon, the Napo, in remote Ecuador. From the Napo eight of us, all but one Vietnam War veterans, pushed and poled a 3,500-pound dugout six days up the Paushi-Yaco and Chapano rivers, through the Auca Indian territory, into an aquatic land never seen by outsiders. What we found and how we survived are the heart of the 2,500-word piece that has already been in print five times in the United States. Three sample slides in the enclosed slide holder, with captions, of the 50 available, show how the excitement and danger are brought to life on the page.

The second, "The Jungle Opera House," is centered on the famed Manaus opera house—1,000 miles up the Amazon—which is being gutted and rebuilt, true to the original in every detail—except that the new house will have rest rooms for the audience and performers! I was given three hours to roam inside, camera in hand, to record the rebuilding. To that I have added the lore, laughs, and location of a cultural monument in one of the world's wildest cities. Three more sample slides appear in the slide holder, with captions, of the 60 available for your choice.

And the third, "Rafting on the Ocean Sea," is an adventure

I stumbled into, a trip 20 miles into the Atlantic Ocean from Salinópolis, Brazil, near the mouth of the Amazon, on a flat raft, a *jangada* like those brought with the slaves from Africa in the 1500s. The purpose? To catch marlin! The problem, though, is that sharks cruise a few feet away, you are usually ankle-deep in water as waves bathe the deck, and how do you keep from slipping off? The article and the last three sample slides (of 60 available) tell all!

If any or all of these interest you for sale abroad, just let me know and I will send the additional slides (indicate the quantity) for your selection.

I also have material, three articles each, about Iceland and England. Are you interested?

Gordon Burgett

Cover Letter 6: Syndication Cover Letter

Purpose. This letter combines elements of both cover and query letters. It is a cover letter because it accompanies actual manuscripts and offers them for reprint. The last paragraph has a query pitch in it, though syndication letters as often solicit interest in a future trip or article as they try to sell material in unused markets.

First paragraph. It's right to the point: Amazon stories for sale outside North America because I am still working the latter market. No reason to dance about with syndicates. Tell them what you have and what you propose, so they can dispose.

Second through fourth paragraphs. Three paragraphs, three articles: you get a few sentences to bring each offering to life. Since you're sending copies of the articles with this letter, these sentences should make the editor want to read each one. Focus on what makes the pieces unique and interesting and why they should be bought from you—now.

Photos. In this case I am sending three samples of slides, with captions, of each story in a slide holder, with an indication of what else I can send later if the editor's interested. Naturally I've picked nine top slides. Teasers. Sometimes syndicates will sell just the slides, but that's extremely rare. Without photography of some sort, a travel-related piece is seldom bought.

In Retrospect

This is the lazy way to sell overseas, and it is only mildly effective. Letters like this one work well within that framework, although you could do a page about each article. I'm not sure the extra time and writing is justified in terms of the extra sales, though. If a syndication editor can't be coaxed in a paragraph to read what's at hand, a page probably won't do any better.

Cover Letter 7

123 Main Street
Santa Maria, CA 93456
(805) 123-4567
Month 1, Year

Ms. Katie Sara Lange
Filler Editor, *Nautical News*
888 Sea Lane
Baleia, ME 00100

Dear Ms. Lange:

There's seldom a reason to send a cover letter with a filler, but I thought it prudent to explain how I know that some of the world's best-known seafarers suffered badly and often from seasickness.

Prince Henry the Navigator, reputed father of oceanic exploration through his "school" at Sagres, Portugal, went to the sea once and nevermore. This fact appears in three writings of the time, one original and two copies that I reviewed in the Greenleaf Collection in Chicago. (I read Portuguese fluently.) In one text he describes the effects of seasickness and says that is why his voyages were on paper, not on board.

Admiral Nelson, of the British fleet, complained regularly in his memoirs of his weak stomach and the despair he faced each time the anchor was lifted, calling his "sea sickness" a test of his love for his country.

And John Paul Jones, like Nelson, considered it the cost of a naval life and spoke of it regularly, from which it passed into reputable history texts.

I'll gladly provide the tomes, pages, and citations, if you wish, but felt it best to simply set your mind at ease that though the filler seems contrary to fact, it is only contrary to what most imagine. Which is what makes it an interesting filler!

Gordon Burgett

Cover Letter 7: Filler Cover Letter

Purpose. Sometimes fillers seem contrary to fact and it makes sense to set the editor's mind at rest with a short (or even long) note to reassure, in this case Ms. Lange, that your items are based on something more than contrariness or wishful thinking.

So here we tell how we know about Prince Henry, Admiral Nelson, and John Paul Jones. Even better, cite the most reliable source or two in each case.

Alas, the seasickness of Prince Henry and Admiral Nelson is true and easily proved, but I made it up for John Paul Jones, just to give you an example! I couldn't stoop to providing that third source—a fictional one at that—and have some poor soul spend months scouring stacks looking for it for a master's thesis. Even cover letter writers have scruples! (Fortunately, scruples aren't as bad as seasickness!)

Incidentally, I could have added, to those with motion sickness (of which seasickness is a liquid variety), Lawrence of Arabia, who was afflicted on camels, and one of my daughters, in a car. But why would the readers of *Nautical News* care?

Cover Letter 8

---

123 Main Street
Santa Maria, CA 93456
(805) 123-4567
Month 1, Year

Mr. Ron Damron
Managing Editor, *The Sightseer*
775 Wabash Avenue
Chicago, IL 60000

Dear Mr. Damron:

An article about Providencia, the Caribbean island near Nicaragua but belonging to Colombia, is enclosed, along with 48 slides (and captions) for your selection.

I'm including this note to share some additional information I discovered in Providencia.

As the article explains, Morgan, the pirate, used Providencia as his port. Since the 1600s, treasure has been sought on and around the island. Two years back the first results of that search came when remains of a ship were found under the sand only 100 yards from the present dock, and a chest that contained Spanish coins was brought up. That is elaborated upon in the article.

What I discovered is that Mrs. Betty Dowd, widow of the crew chief that extracted the chest, has some 40 excellent

---

slides of the item being removed from the water, opened on the shore, and the coins being cleaned and inspected. She let me view the slides and promised that she would make them available to me if you were interested in using one for the cover.

Based on the cover rate stated in last year's *Writer's Market*, I told her that if one was used she could expect $200. (That was the first question she asked!) Naturally I made no promise for their use, and I explained that if you were interested, you would have to see at least 20 slides from which to select one. I picked the best 20, left her a heavy plastic slide holder, and showed her how to insure and register the mailing to me.

Frankly, I think they are super shots, have never been used before, and would frame the article perfectly. But it's up to you. If you're interested, let me know. I'll call her, and I can have these in your hands within about a week from that time. No word from you and I'll drop her a thank-you note in about a month.

Let me know if I can be of further assistance.

Gordon Burgett

Cover Letter 8: Photo Cover Letter

Purpose: first and second paragraphs. In this example I've just finished writing an article about Providencia for *The Sightseer*, in response to a query and am submitting it with this cover letter.

Normally there is no need for a cover to accompany a queried manuscript submission—unless there is something unique or particular to note or add. Here I want to add something, and I explain it in the first two paragraphs.

Third paragraph. To understand the importance of what I found it is necessary to restate a key point in the article: that Morgan's treasure has been sought since the 1600s on this small island—and that treasure was indeed found within sight of the main pier just two years back!

Fourth paragraph. But I made a discovery of my own. Slides of that treasure being removed exist; they are excellent, and they have never been used. Ideal for the cover! Best yet, I can get them for the editor's review.

Fifth and sixth paragraphs. The details. Money. When the editor can get them. How they will be sent.

Seventh paragraph. On the other hand, there may just be a cover gem in my 48 slides that accompany this letter. Finding Morgan's gold was a miracle—and it was close at hand. So are my slides.

In Retrospect

I've sold plenty of photos found during research in just this way, so it works. Editors appreciate it too, though they'd rather not have you bandy about their fees as I had to do here. A cover letter is also a good way to tell where you found the best historical pictures in the texts you consulted, each with the author, title, edition, page number, and photo credit listed.

Cover Letter 9

123 Main Street
Santa Maria, CA 93456
(805) 123-4567
Month 1, Year

Mr. Ira Cyril
Editor, *World Business News*
7818 Grafton Street
Boston, MA 08000

Dear Mr. Cyril:

Sorry for the two-week delay in getting this article in your hands.

As you recall from our phone conversation about three weeks back, my interview with Cedric Johnstone was postponed because of an urgent trip he had to make to China and Japan on State Department business.

The interview, held last Tuesday in New York City, was far more informative, though, because of the trip, and I think the article shows that.

In fact, if you're interested, it opens up the possibility of an intriguing sidebar or box on China's growing interest in Japan's establishment of an automated computer production plant in China itself. Mr. Johnstone gave me some specific facts about this, plus three names I can contact for further information. I'd need about a week to bring it together. Please let me know if you are interested, a preferred length, any specific info you desire, and a deadline. Or would this article be better for a future issue?

I'll gladly provide source validation for any of the points made or facts cited.

Let me know if I can be of further assistance.

Gordon Burgett

Cover Letter 9: Delayed Submission Cover Letter

Purpose: first and second paragraphs. In this case I had queried the editor of *World Business News* and expected to have the copy in his hands in three weeks. But late in the second week my interview with a key person central to the article had to be postponed. I called Mr. Cyril, explained the situation, and asked for a delay until that interview could be completed.

Now I am submitting the final manuscript, plus a cover letter reminding him of our previous telephone conversation and some information specific to that postponed interview.

Third paragraph. It gives this cover letter extra yardage. Mind you, most would end after the first two paragraphs and a courteous closing. But here I have a possibility of adding to the article being sent (for an additional payment) or the core of a later article. So I give the information needed about a sidebar—basic facts, some idea of the sources, and when it can be sent. And I leave open the possibility of being asked to send a fuller query about a later article if the editor is interested.

Thoughts

It is rare that you must delay manuscript submissions so a letter like this one must be written to meet a particular situation. Use common sense. It's just a courtesy letter anyway. Sometimes it opens up additional sales.

Cover Letter 10

123 Main Street
Santa Maria, CA 93456
(805) 123-4567
Month 1, Year

Ms. Mary Ann Farrens
Fiction Editor, Hansun House Publishers
1738 Broadway
New York, NY 10000

Dear Ms. Farrens:

I am submitting three chapters and a synopsis of my latest novel, *White Gold*, as suggested in the current *Writer's Market*. (My previous three were published by Albany Woods Press, which no longer handles fiction.)

Three additional factors might particularly interest you, Ms. Farrens, or the Hansun House marketing director, and they may not be apparent from simply reading the texts, thus this short cover letter.

First, "white gold" refers to a form of sap from a rare palm tree found only in the Oriente area of Ecuador where the Paushi-Yaco and Chapano rivers meet. Its curative powers are well-known in the medical world, as they were to the northernmost group of Indians conquered by the Incas.

Second, its value tops $3,000 a liter. The sap has drawn to this primitive area at least six groups, really gangs, hell-bent on extracting every last ounce for commercial sale. The result is predictable: Gang wars have left scores dead in this lawless jungle. At the same time the gangs are wiping out a fierce group of Indians called the Aucas. And the trees themselves, sensitive to excessive tapping, may well be totally eliminated before scientists can get in to save some of them for planting and cultivation elsewhere.

Third, what I have told you is true. I was liaison member with a U.N. task force attempting to enter the area to effect just such a preservation. The news of this sap, its nearly miraculous powers on malignancies and growth deformations, and the plight of the palm and those attempting to save it will hit the news soon.

The book, as these chapters show, puts the story into a slightly fictionalized context to permit a better look at the gangs, about which virtually nothing is otherwise known. But the rest, except the names and a few modifications to protect actual people, is true. It makes super reading because it's so damned tragic.

If you think it merits publication, let me know quickly and I can have the rest of the text in your hands in 10 days. Then when the news pops, so do you.

If you have any questions, please write or call.

Gordon Burgett

Cover Letter 10: Cover Letter for a Novel

Purpose. To tell Ms. Farrens why my novel is particularly timely and why the lucky publisher who rushes it into print will be in the chips when the subject about which it is written hits the news!

First and second paragraphs. A quick explanation of why I'm sending a cover letter along with the chapters and synopsis. I also slipped in a plug that I've already had three novels in print.

Third through sixth paragraphs. Here's the subject and why it will be in the newspapers and on TV—and why, by implication, my book will be hot material for a movie or TV special. Without this rather elaborate background, the book's just another hacker's dream, another so many pages in the pile to be read if and when somebody gets to it. And probably to be rejected as being too farfetched—too far from reality yet not far enough to be a *Star Wars*. So I draw a special look by sending it with a special cover letter.

Seventh paragraph. If Ms. Farrens believes the first six paragraphs and likes what she sees in skimming the synopsis and chapters that accompany the letter, she may well ask to see the whole book—today, sent air express! So the book's in print before the news!

In Retrospect

It's a good way to get special attention for your novel. But you can't fake it. There should be a reason for writing the cover letter, other than your desperation to get into print and get rich.

Incidentally, do you believe that malarkey about the rare palm tree's sap and its super cures? Sorry. I couldn't even sell that to Hansun House, since they are as fictional as the plot. The only thing that is real is Mary Ann Farrens. She's my step-aunt and a sweet gal. But since she's from Missouri and a school teacher, I couldn't even sell it to Mary Ann, cover letter or not.

APPENDIX C

Ten More Query Letters

I've added 10 more query letters. In substance and form, they vary hardly at all from the way I would have written them 5 or 15 years back. Except that the topics, as close as I can guess, are what today's magazine readers want to know about. In fact, most of the topics are rather timeless and universal, but tied into today's life. And they are topics that I care about. Why waste your energy writing about things that, to you, are either unimportant or at least uninteresting? Sometimes you don't have that luxury, but given a choice and time, as magazines afford you, why not pick subjects that make a difference?

My article writing has largely been replaced by book writing, so most of these queries were never sent. Rather, I have selected the magazine I would initially send them to, written them precisely as I would were I to follow up with the research and composition, and put them in final query form. Should the ideas interest you, pursue them yourself. (But, of course, create your own query!)

What we have, then, are 10 ideas that might help put you in print, suggested in final query form.

Query Letter 11

123 Main Street
Santa Maria, CA 93456
(805) 123-4567
Month 1, Year

Editorial/Features Editor
American Health Magazine
28 W. 23rd Street
New York, NY 10010

Dear Editor:

There's no genetic reason why women should outlive men at all, much less 6.9 years or more. It's an American phenomenon of this century. And it's the other way around in much of the Third World.

The idea for my article isn't that female longevity should be reduced, but that we should finally face the question of why American males needlessly die younger. Better said, why does their machismo deprive them of the better part of a decade of life—years more of vital, healthy living?

Marvin Harris, in *Our Kind*, puts his finger on the modifiable social and medical causes: "Males smoke more cigarettes than women, eat more fatty red meat, drink more alcohol, take more hard drugs, expose themselves to more industrial poisons and on-the-job hazards, drive faster and more recklessly, possess more firearms and other deadly weapons, and more often acquire tension-building competitive personalities."

The result? More heart attacks, strokes, cardiovascular diseases, lung cancer, cirrhosis of the liver, car and job accidents, murder, and suicide.

The topic begs a hard look at the related statistics, genes, and social history with a half-dozen experts to see why this thesis flies in the face of current supposition. We should grasp the causes and solution—not as cold academic facts but through exposition, quote, and anecdote to create an article that makes a difference.

Ignorance and early death are a hard price for men to pay for outdrinking, outdriving, and outdoing their buddies because "that's what it takes to be a man." I've been in print well over 1,000 times. Should we peel back some of that ignorance on your pages so your subscribers can live longer?

Thanks.

Gordon Burgett

Query Letter 12

123 Main Street
Santa Maria, CA 93456
(805) 123-4567
Month 1, Year

Nonfiction Editor, *Sports Parade*
Meridian Publishing Co., Inc.
P.O. Box 10010
Ogden, UT 84409

Dear Nonfiction Editor:

Your readers must be as shocked and dumbfounded as I am when a young stud signs a contract for $5 million a year just to play baseball! For hitting and running and fielding the way we did a few years back—but better. Five million dollars better?

I'd like to help your readers better understand just what those contracts mean. And who ultimately pays. Plenty of facts, but anecdotes and examples and big names too, gleaned through interviews with the major league clubs, agents, and players—with help from other sportswriter friends.

For example, how is that $5 million paid? When? Is there any tax protection? Who pays if the player gets hurt? Does he earn a per diem on the road, for hotels and food, in addition to the contract? What happens if he's traded? When the team makes a commercial, does he get part of the kitty? If he makes one, does some of that go into the team kitty? Does any of the contract amount go into the veterans' fund? How much goes to the agent and other intermediaries? Does the team write other, nonplaying services into the agreement?

As to who pays, how much of the money for these contracts comes from the admission costs? Or the concessions? Do one or several giant contracts mean that the rest of the team earns less? Or is the team inferior in quality because management can't pay more to more support players?

You get the idea. And the readers finally get a handle on how much take-home money $5 million means, as well as how many cents their tickets put in the player's pocket. Best yet, you get a $5 million article for *Sports Parade* for much less!

I've been in print 1,000-plus times. Once more, on your pages, with this nuts-and-bolts piece?

Thanks.

Gordon Burgett

Query Letter 13

123 Main Street
Santa Maria, CA 93456
(805) 123-4567
Month 1, Year

Mr. Jim Rosenthal
Editor, *Men's Fitness*
21100 Erwin Street
Woodland Hills, CA 91367

Dear Mr. Rosenthal:

Hemorrhoids are a pain in the you-know-what. And most people have them, which, by extension, includes more than half of your readers.

So let me prepare a state-of-the-art article about the topic for those readers, using the "h" word openly, though with anatomical discretion—and occasional, appropriate humor.

What do most people want to know? What hemorrhoids really are, which of the many over-the-counter medications and ointments work, and when is it necessary to go to the doctor for more powerful aids. As well as what can be done in the dietary, hygienic, and sitz bath area to lessen their effect or prevent them altogether.

Are they ever dangerous? What else might the commonly related bleeding indicate? When might an otherwise healthy person expect this itchy, irksome affliction?

The most exciting news comes in the area of hemorrhoidectomy and ligation, where the painful and costly methods of the past are giving way to quicker, less expensive means, including the injection of shrinking agents, freezing by cryosurgery, manual stretching, and even applying rubber bands on an outpatient basis to wither the devils away.

Sources? Mainly four key doctors in this field from different parts of the country, plus background info from current medical texts. Add to that the comments of three everyday people who are no longer afflicted, and we have the heart of a helpful, informative, and even amusing piece. Alas, I don't suggest photos this time.

I've already been in print 1,000-plus times. Don't be offended that I picked your publication for this topic! But isn't it time we shared the good news about it with your silently suffering readers?

Thanks.

Gordon Burgett

Query Letter 14

---

123 Main Street
Santa Maria, CA 93456
(805) 123-4567
Month 1, Year

Ms. Connie Kurz
Food and Family Issues
USA Weekend
Gannett Co. Inc.
Box 500-W
Washington, DC 20044

Dear Ms. Kurz:

Twins: Double the trouble or double the fun? One in about 90 is a twin, and all of your readers know a twin. Mirror twins write with different hands, identical males usually get bald or fat in the same way at about the same time, and blacks win the prize for having twins most often. . . .

That's what I'd like to write for your pages, a fun piece full of "twin" facts for which you needn't pay me twice as much. Why do I care? Because I am one: identical, with a brother six minutes younger, and eight inches taller. Religiously we're miles apart, yet we have the same IQs. So I got interested.

Some of the piece will contain the basics: fraternal (two out of three) versus identical, and the suspected "half-identical," found in flatworms and sea urchins yet still unproven in humans. "Siamese twins." Identity problems. Famous twins: Jacob and Esau, Remus and Romulus (for whom Rome was named), the Doublemint duo, Jody and Buffy in "The Family Affair," skiers Phil and Steve Mahre, Abigail Van Buren and Ann Landers, and the ageless Bobbsey twins. Don't forget the Gemini sign, Shakespeare's *Comedy of Errors* (he fathered twins), Dumas' *The Man in the Iron Mask,* Hayley Mills in *The Parent Trap,* and the world's most unlikely linking, Arnold Schwarzenegger and Danny DeVito.

The rest would be scientifically intriguing, from the two forms of "twin testing." One is the conventional system of comparing identical and fraternal twins to see the importance of heredity versus environment. The other is a look at identical twins separated from birth to see how completely different environments acted on genetic similarities. I'd go to the documented studies here and include interviewed comments from their authors.

That's it: A general interest item in the nature-versus-nurture sense that affects us all. I've been in print 1,000-plus times. Hope my chances are better than 1:90 with *USA Weekend.* Just let me know!

Gordon Burgett

Query Letter 15

123 Main Street
Santa Maria, CA 93456
(805) 123-4567
Month 1, Year

Mr. Bill Strickland
Submissions Editor, *Writer's Digest*
1507 Dana Avenue
Cincinnati, OH 45207

Dear Mr. Strickland:

If your readers have a book in them and want to earn at least $50,000 profit from it, and then double that, they need to read the article I want to write for your pages.

Snake oil? Nope! Niche publishing. With the technology and tools now available to everyone—computers, hands-on software, laser printing—and a huge thirst for usable information priming the economy, those who can target this information first, customize it to that specifically targeted market, and then expand its availability by related means are at the heart of publishing's coming breakthrough.

I wrote the only book about niche publishing, *Self-Publishing to Tightly-Targeted Markets*, and released it for sale about a year back. (Mrs. Mert Ransdell bought it for the WD Book Club then, the fourth book of mine on writing to be sold by your firm that way.) Yet I've never shared this information through articles, even though I've had more than 1,000 other articles in print. So here's a chance for your readers to learn about the TCE (target, customize, and expand) process first on your pages!

There were 470 publishers in 1946 and there are about 21,000 today. By the year 2000 that number will nearly quintuple, to 100,000. The number of standard, big-volume publishers probably won't increase much above 1,000. Most of the rest will be niche publishers. Shouldn't we help your readers be the first to learn about this new philosophy and process, through a step-by-step article that covers all the bases, by explanation and through an easy-to-follow example, plus of course examples of others who have made the process work?

I'm sending with this letter two PR sheets that I usually send to book reviewers, Mr. Strickland. These sheets explain the concept in greater detail. I'm also sending a copy of the book for your use. (Please keep it, give it to another book writing friend, or donate it to your library.)

Books are usually articles writ long. Most of your readers are article writers, so in terms of interest they are first in line for this kind of how-to information. Niche publishing is a bountifully nutritious supper to feed your hungry subscribing horde. Should I start cooking?

Please let me know. And thanks.

Gordon Burgett

Query Letter 16

123 Main Street
Santa Maria, CA 93456
(805) 123-4567
Month 1, Year

Articles Editor, *Parade Magazine*
Parade Publications, Inc.
750 Third Avenue
New York, NY 10017

Dear Articles Editor:

All of us die eventually, even your readers. But what they do with their bodies, or parts of them, differs from person to person and can be determined while they are still alive—usually.

That's what I want to share on your pages. An informative article about donating bodies (one's own!) and their parts, with a how-to segment at the end (or, excuse me, in a box), including plenty of examples, quotes, and—yes—even humor, appropriately spread.

Topics the article would cover are (1) why you would even consider donating your body, (2) who can do it, (3) who you can contact about it, (4) how does anybody know of your wishes if you die far from home, (5) who will take a body badly ravaged by disease or accident, (6) can you donate different parts to various organizations and the body (or what's left) to another group, (7) what use is made of donated bodies, (8) what is done with the remains later, and (9) what happens after you have died if you wanted to donate but your family (or anybody else) objects?

Sound macabre? People are far more realistic than they were just 20 years ago when I went through the process of donating mine to a university—later. Some of my family were aghast; others assured me the university wouldn't take my body when they saw it! But now they too are asking the same questions, at least about eyes, hearts, and internal organs. It's really in response to their questions to me that I became aware of the need for sharing this information with a greater audience. Like the readers of your pages, may they live and subscribe long.

Ready to share valuable information about how some of your *Parade Magazine* readers can, in a sense, continue to live beyond death, or at least contribute in a very material way to gathering knowledge that will help their grandchildren's grandchildren?

I've had 1,000-plus articles in print. We'd better add this one to the tally before that university makes its claim!

Gordon Burgett

Query Letter 17

123 Main Street
Santa Maria, CA 93456
(805) 123-4567
Month 1, Year

Ms. Ande Zellman
Editor-in-Chief, *Boston Globe Magazine*
135 Morrissey Boulevard
Boston, MA 02107

Dear Ms. Zellman:

Do your readers want to learn a doubly useful foreign language? Forget Chinese—too many other people speak it. French? Maybe for poets. Spanish? In Massachusetts, go one better: Learn Portuguese!

Yep, the tongue of everybody's household hero, Luiz Vaz de Camões. The language about which Philip II, king of the entire Iberian peninsula, said, "Give me my commerce in Spanish, my poetry and song in Portuguese!" Yet the language sounds as if the speaker just smelled something moldy, its lyrical verses clipped by contractions and blown half through the nose. . . .

Let's have some factual fun with your readers and still share a helpful clue: If they learn Portuguese, they also learn Spanish. Since Portuguese has twice as many working words, Spanish is in there. It's the way those words are said that gives people two tongues for the price of learning one.

Anyway, every ship needs somebody aboard who speaks English or Portuguese, the second language of the sea. (Any wonder that Annapolis has one of the best Portuguese language departments in the United States?) Whether you land in Brazil (where more than half the inhabitants of South America live), Macao, Africa (Angola or Mozambique, mainly), Diu or Goa in India, or even the motherland itself, you will understand and be understood perfectly. But not along the Rio San Francisco in northern Brazil, where locals still recite as everyday words Camões' great epic poem *Os Lusiadas*, written in the late 1500s, which, to us, would be about as unlikely as finding a West Virginian conversationally reciting *Beowulf*—from memory.

Where would *Moby Dick* be without the Portuguese whalers from New Bedford, and where would France's Edith Piaf have found her baleful music without the Portuguese *fados*, wailing in song about those whaling men? Where would Formosa have gotten its name? Where would we have gotten the samba, or the phrase "taking the bull by the horns"?

There's much, much more of the mystery and majesty of the Portuguese tongue that I'd like to wrap humorously into an article of about 1,500 words to delight your readers. Ready? I've been in print 1,000-plus times. Let me know if you're interested, with my thanks.

Gordon Burgett

Query Letter 18

123 Main Street
Santa Maria, CA 93456
(805) 123-4567
Month 1, Year

Mr. Ian Ledgerwood
Editor-in-Chief, *Modern Maturity Magazine*
AARP
3200 E. Carson
Lakewood, CA 90712

Dear Mr. Ledgerwood:

On the front of my first greeting card there was a nebbish sitting atop a heart, asking the question, "Why should I wait until Valentine's to tell you how I feel?"

Inside it said, "I feel fine, thank you."

Yes, a groaner. But Hallmark loved it, paid me $50, and has continued selling it for at least 15 years! That was many, many hundreds of cards ago—and it began more than 1,000 articles back.

Let's show your readers how they too can tap that fun market, earn a return for the lines only (close to $100 apiece now), and even later convert sold cards into cartoons, bumper stickers, and buttons. All legit, writing and submitting and keeping records like professionals, all of whom started the way I'll explain.

There used to be a great book that led me and others through the process called *The Guide to Greeting Card Writing*. But it's out of print forever, nothing has replaced it, and my tape series "Writing Comedy Greeting Cards That Sell!" (from a four-hour fun writing seminar I give throughout California) is all that's around. So let's save your readers $24.95 + and let me share the steps, fun, and excitement on your pages.

No artwork is required for commercial submissions—a blessing for those like me who can draw only flies. The companies have in-house cartoon folk who see how to double the comedic impact of our lines. (Only rarely must you explain what should be drawn to make the joke work; I'll show how and when that's done.) The writer conjures up a dozen funny lines, batches and records them, and off they go—on cards a special size and weight. It's easy and fun once you know what the buyer expects.

Incidentally, I'll use my own selling cards as examples so we have no permissions to get. Except yours, to write these lines for your pages. Ready?

Gordon Burgett

Query Letter 19

123 Main Street
Santa Maria, CA 93456
(805) 123-4567
Month 1, Year

Ms. Caryne Brown
Editor, *Women's Enterprise for Entrepreneurs*
Paisano Publications, Inc.
28210 Dorothy Drive
Agoura, CA 91301

Dear Ms. Brown:

If your readers are interested in earning good money by sharing information, both now and as consultants later, they should seriously consider offering seminars or workshops!

Seminars, in a generic sense, are the bright light of the educational future. Professionals have already been to college; they don't want classes week after week, parking hassles, health center fees, and the rest of it. They want immediately applicable information tightly packaged, well explained, and reinforced with a solid workbook. All in one session, a night or a weekend. Learning in usable, affordable bite sizes.

Let's help your readers get on the giving/earning side of this enterprise, said to reap from $3 billion to $10 billion annually! I wrote *Speaking for Money* a few years back; half of that tells how to create seminars. At present I offer 120 seminars annually in California, probably more than any other person. One of my favorites is "How to Set Up and Market Your Own Seminar," also the title of a three-tape series by the same name.

Let me draw from those sources, tailor make an article for your female readers, then fill it with facts, how-to steps, examples, and quotes.

Best yet, colleges and universities are eager to add practical new courses to their offerings. So are associations. Some seminars are best given self-sponsored, at hotels or halls centrally located to a wide range of participants. Finally, companies hunt for good programs that will help their employees do everything from greeting customers to writing memos.

That's the heart of it. A lot of your readers know things, ways, and processes that others would eagerly pay to learn. That's where seminars start. Let's help those readers convert that knowledge into income so the rest of us can benefit too!

I've been in print 1,000-plus times, and this article seems like a natural for your pages. Just let me know, with my thanks in advance.

Gordon Burgett

Query Letter 20

123 Main Street
Santa Maria, CA 93456
(805) 123-4567
Month 1, Year

Ms. Leifa Butrick
Editor, *Singlelife Magazine*
606 W. Wisconsin Avenue
Milwaukee, WI 53203

Dear Ms. Butrick:

Is there anything more perplexing to a starving single than a package of frozen meat and an empty microwave oven? Let's unravel this tragedy in a fun, fact-filled article in *Singlelife Magazine*.

Whether you're thrust anew into culinary survival, as millions of marital castoffs like me are annually, or if you escape from home for the first time—hungry and truly unschooled—iced meat and heat do not a meal make!

What I propose is a humorous look at the very basics, like five meats—chicken, steak, pork chops, hamburger, and ribs—and two simple, tasty recipes for each, starting with what you seek in the supermarket, what you don't wrap in foil in the microwave, and why you don't invite your true love to your first bout with ribs sauté. Meals for Monday through Friday, leftovers on Sunday, and real food in a restaurant on Saturday—a reward for having outlived your own scullery concoctions!

It took me a year to get it right. But I had help: lots of cooking classes, a great old aunt who could bake a salted shoe that would make your mouth water, and a food critic friend who helped me pick out 10 recipes that any idiot could fix and any sweetheart would swoon to share.

Isn't it time we brought your readers some of this simple cooking savvy? I've been in print 1,000-plus times elsewhere. Ready for a taste of Gordon Burgett's favorite dish: fun in print, flambéed, with a purpose?

Thanks.

                                              Gordon Burgett

GLOSSARY

Angle. An approach to an idea or subject, a point of view, a way of researching a topic and writing about it for print. For example, an article about a professional baseball player as seen by the batboy.

Approach. See angle. A way of seeing a topic and writing about it for print.

Assignment. An understanding or a contract in which an editor asks a writer to prepare and submit an article or book, often with specific stipulations about length, due date, and payment.

B/w. Black-and-white photograph. Also b&w.

Flush left, ragged right. In this book the margins of the query or cover letter. In flush left, the left margin is vertically aligned. In ragged right, the right margin is irregular.

Go-ahead. A positive reply to a query letter telling the writer to prepare and submit the manuscript and that the editor will seriously consider the finished piece for publication. Usually means the work is performed on speculation.

ms/mss. Abbreviations for manuscript and manuscripts. Also MS/MSS.

Package. Editors often consider and buy manuscripts and illustrations together, as a "package."

Pix. Pictures; photos and/or slides.

Proofsheets. The negative strips are laid on a contact sheet and the whole roll is developed, with each photo the same size as the negative. Often used instead of enlarged photographic prints.

Reprint. An item that reappears in print, as is or with few substantive changes, after it was originally published by someone else. Reprint rights and second rights are the same thing. Reprints usually require an accompanying cover letter when submitted for sale.

Rewrites. Using one article as the base, a rewrite generally includes much of the same contents but deletes or adds information and/or alters the order of the original contents to produce a different article.

SASE. Self-addressed, stamped envelope.

Slant. See angle. A way of seeing or approaching a topic and writing about it for print.

Speculation When "writing on speculation" the freelancer writes on the understanding that the editor is not committed to buy the item or pay a fee if it isn't used.

Tearsheets. Literally, pages torn from a magazine or newspaper containing the writer's printed copy. Photocopies of the original work are acceptable in this modern age.

BIBLIOGRAPHY

Biagi, Shirley, *How to Write & Sell Magazine Articles.* Prentice-Hall, 1989.

Burgett, Gordon, *How to Sell More Than 75% of Your Freelance Writing.* Prima Publishing, 1990.

Burgett, Gordon, *Ten Sales from One Article Idea: The Process and Correspondence.* Write to Sell, 1982.

Collier, Oscar, and Frances Leighton, *How to Write and Sell Your First Nonfiction Book.* St. Martin's Press, 1990.

Cool, Lisa Collier, *How to Sell Every Magazine Article You Write.* Writer's Digest Books, 1989.

Cool, Lisa Collier, *How to Write Irresistible Query Letters.* Writer's Digest Books, 1988.

Enos, Sondra F., *Breaking into Article Writing.* The Writer, 1988.

Higgins, George V., *On Writing: Advice for Those Who Want to Publish.* Holt and Co., 1990.

Kozar, Ellen, *From Pen to Print: The Secret of Getting Published Successfully.* Holt and Co., 1990.

Meredith, Scott, *Writing to Sell.* Harper and Row, 1982.

Newcomb, Duane, *How to Sell and Re-Sell Your Writing.* Writer's Digest Books, 1987.

Potter, Clarkson, *Writing for Publication.* Harper and Row, 1990.

Writer's Market, current edition. Writer's Digest Books.

INDEX

OTHER BOOKS FROM THE
GORDON BURGETT LIBRARY

Gordon Burgett books and audiocassette tapes have helped tens of thousands of writers and speakers prosper. Here are his hand-picked titles selected especially for readers of this book.

BOOKS

Self-Publishing to Tightly-Targeted Markets

Subtitled "How to Earn $50,000 from Your First Book—Then Double It!," this book shows you how to identify and reach buyers who need specific information and are willing to pay almost anything to get it. Includes all you need to know, from book production to marketing. $14.95

Empire-Building by Writing and Speaking

If you have an exciting idea, you can have power—provided you learn how to increase your sphere of influence through writing and speaking. By widening your circle of influence, your income will multiply, sometimes a hundred times. Here are all the techniques necessary to take your idea, seminar, or expertise and make it your guide to a six- or even seven-figure income. $15.95

The Travel Writer's Guide

This book demystifies the process and explains in a step-by-step method how virtually anyone who is literate can earn from travel writing. Burgett's three-step action plan takes travel writers through the before-, during-, and after-travel phases. $14.95

Ten Sales from One Article Idea

"Burgett has written a precise, step-by-step blueprint for getting published, one that even the novice ought to use with expectation of success . . . a valuable addition to any writer's library." *Palos Verdes View* (CA) $7.95

ORDER FORM

Please send me the following items:

Quantity	Title	Unit Price	Total
_____	_____	$____	$____
_____	_____	$____	$____
_____	_____	$____	$____
_____	_____	$____	$____

Subtotal $_____

7.25% SALES TAX (California only) .... $_____

SHIPPING ($3 for the first item, $1.50 for each
additional item) .... $_____

TOTAL ORDER .... $_____

HOW TO ORDER

By telephone: With Visa/MC, call (916) 786-0426, Mon.–Fri.,
9–4 PST.

By mail: Just fill out the information below and send with your
remittance.

I am paying by (check one): ☐ Check ☐ Money Order
☐ Visa/MC

My name is _____

I live at _____

City _____ State _____ Zip _____

Visa/MC # _____ Exp. _____

Signature _____

PRIMA PUBLISHING
P.O. Box 1260B3
Rocklin, CA 95677
(Satisfaction unconditionally guaranteed)

How to Sell More Than 75% of Your Freelance Writing

Amateurs write, then try to sell. . . . Professionals sell, then write. This is the theme of this revised and updated edition of Gordon Burgett's landmark book on the business of selling what you write. $12.95

AUDIOCASSETTES

Here are the recordings of some of Gordon Burgett's own seminars before an audience of his students. If they include areas of interest to you, you will find them of immense and permanent value as you listen to them again and again.

Writing Travel Articles that Sell! (3 tapes) $39.95
Before You Write Your Nonfiction Book
  (3 tapes) $39.95
Writing Comedy Greeting Cards that Sell
  (2 tapes) $24.95
How to Self-Publish and Market Your Own Book
  (3 tapes) $44.95
Producing and Selling Your Own Audio-Cassette
  (1 tape) $9.95

Also Available from Prima Publishing

The Insider's Guide to Book Editors, Publishers and Literary Agents—1992–1993 Edition, by Jeff Herman

Updated annually. Here is the most comprehensive listing of book publishers and the names of editors and their specialty within each publishing house. Over 250 houses are included as well as the most complete information by top experts on what it takes to be successfully published. New to this edition are extensive details about more than 125 powerful literary agents. $18.95
And don't forget to order additional copies of
The Writer's Guide to Query Letters and Cover
  Letters $12.95